I cannot remember the last time I read a book on union with Christ and was so convicted that I stopped and prayed. But that is exactly what happened when I read the book by Ken Berding you hold in your hands. Without compromising biblical and theological depth, Berding unveils the innumerable ways union with Christ makes a real difference in the Christian life. Not only will Berding clarify who you are as a Christian but he will help you know how to live like a Christian. Through his own experience as a professor, missionary, husband, and father, Berding will open your eyes to the centrality of union with Christ.

Matthew Barrett
Associate Professor of Christian Theology,
Midwestern Baptist Theological Seminary
Executive editor, *Credo Magazine,* and author of *None Greater*

Understanding the meaning and significance of our new identity as believers in relationship to Jesus Christ is the number one concern of the Apostle Paul in his letters. One could say that this is the secret for living the Christian life—although there should be nothing secret about it. Deep prayerful reflection on these key elements of life *in Christ* will transform you from the inside out.

Clinton E. Arnold
Dean and Professor of New Testament, Talbot School of Theology
(Biola University), La Mirada, California

Dr. Berding is at his best in this book, bringing us to the fundamental truths of Scripture and applying them to our lives with relevancy for Christians at all levels of maturity. Meditation on our inChristness refreshes and revitalizes life for the individual Christian and for the church as a whole. Reading this book over the course of 100 days will help you understand your Bible better, settle your daily thoughts in a direction of truthful rest and awaken you to effectively serve the mission of Christ in this world!

Kyle Fox
Lead Pa   urch, Meza, Arizona

D1613024

Theologically rich, yet intensely practical; I felt as if Ken were providing me with a set of 'in Christ' lenses through which to view every facet of my life. I will revisit this book often to refocus my gaze on Christ, and all that is true of life *in Him*.

Jeffrey Bruce
Lead Pastor, Creekside Community Church, San Leandro, California

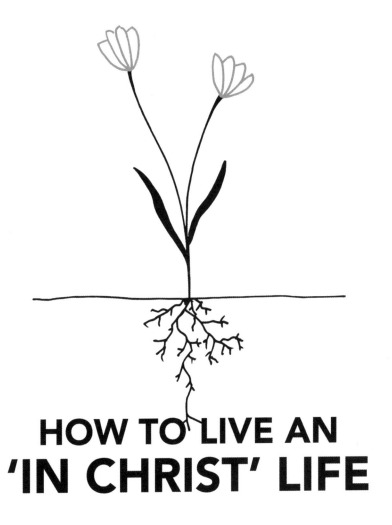

HOW TO LIVE AN 'IN CHRIST' LIFE

100 Devotional Readings
on Union With Christ

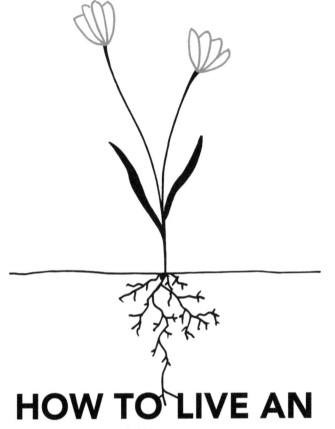

HOW TO LIVE AN
'IN CHRIST' LIFE

KENNETH BERDING

CHRISTIAN
FOCUS

CONTENTS

DAILY LIFE *IN CHRIST*

COMMUNITY AND MISSION *IN CHRIST*

To my children, grandchildren, and great-grandchildren,
whether through birth, fostering, or adoption, born already or
yet-to-be born.
My constant longing and continual prayer is that each of you
might come to know the reality of life *in Christ.*

INTRODUCTION

This book is deeply personal for me. I grew up in a church that under-emphasized the Holy Spirit. Through God's insistent grace and the gradual working of His Word upon my mind and heart I steadily came into a fuller understanding of the work of the Holy Spirit, and started writing about life in the Spirit.[1] An unintended consequence of emphasizing the Bible's teaching about the Holy Spirit was that for a while I found myself somewhat unsure of how to relate daily to *Jesus*, the second person of the Trinity. Let me explain.

In the church where I grew up, since we didn't put proper emphasis on the Holy Spirit, we often filled the hole with Jesus. So we would ask *Jesus* to guide us, or we would ask *Jesus* to convict us of sin, or we would ask *Jesus* to comfort us. But when I discovered that these activities in the Bible often focus upon the third person of the Trinity, the Holy Spirit, there emerged a gap in knowing how to relate personally to Jesus. I already knew how to relate to the first person of the Trinity, God the Father, since I directed my prayers—following the normal pattern of the Bible—toward the Father. Furthermore, I knew and insistently articulated that the central focus of my life, including my daily actions, should center on the honor and glory of God the Father. But what about Jesus? How was I supposed to relate to God the Son on a day-to-day basis?

Prayer highlights the difficulty. What is the role of each person of the Trinity in our praying? Here is the standard Christian response (each statement entirely correct): We pray to the Father, based upon the Son's atoning work, by the power of the Spirit. But notice how personal the roles of the Father and the Spirit are in this equation, whereas how *objective,* or *foundational,* or *positional,* or—dare I say it?—*impersonal* is the role of the Son in this statement.

Please don't misunderstand. I am overwhelmingly and eternally grateful for what Jesus Christ has done on my behalf in taking upon Himself the wrath of God that I deserve and thereby providing access to the Father. I fully, completely, and wholeheartedly believe this. Furthermore, I believe that affirming the objective work of Christ's atoning sacrifice for sinners is central, fundamental, and vital for every Christ-follower. There is salvation in no other name under heaven. I am nothing apart from the cross of Christ. But how do I relate to Jesus today? What about in this moment? Is there something I am missing in relating to Jesus on a daily basis?

InChristness is the answer. Every theologian knows that the concept sometimes referred to as *inChristness* in this book (more commonly called *union with Christ*) is one of the most important topics in the letters of the Apostle Paul. Some scholars go so far as to claim that if you want to understand the mind of Paul, before everything else, you must grasp what he thinks about *this.*

But the implications of understanding *inChristness* go far beyond simply entering into a deeper understanding of Paul. The truths unpacked in this book might just change the way you view your whole life. The implications of grasping *inChristness* are so far-reaching, so soul-searching, so inspiring, and so deep that I can confidently predict that they could be life-changing for you. These truths could rock more areas of your world than the earthquakes we regularly experience in Southern California where I make my home. I hope you are impacted as deeply in reading this book as I have been in writing it. I can testify that my own soul has been encouraged and I have experienced significant spiritual strengthening in the midst of some suffering as I have meditated upon and written the devotionals you are about to read.

The purpose of this book is to uncover and clarify how union with Christ impacts the way we as Christians live out our daily lives. The book is comprised of 100 two-page devotional readings that you can choose to read all at once or over the course of 100 days. You can read them in sequence or select whatever order works best for you. You can read them on your own or pull together a small group and discuss them together. (Note the review questions at the end of the book.) These reflections on life *in Christ* will introduce you to moments in the letters of the Apostle Paul where he connects *inChristness* with daily life. In other words, I intentionally allow Paul himself to lead us in how to apply *inChristness* to the way we walk through life. I only make applications where Paul—under the inspiration of the Holy Spirit—has already suggested applications. My hope is that this approach will provide space for the Spirit of God to help you perceive practical applications for your daily life *in Christ* that have already been made in His holy Word. In preparation for our journey, I invite you to pray the following prayer:

Dear Lord. I deeply desire to know what it means to be in Christ. I want to understand it, internalize it, be changed by it, and increasingly live out an in-Christ life. I ask for a heart to hear, and grace to grow. I pray these things in your name... in Christ. *Amen.*

CHAPTER 1

INCHRISTNESS

'Excuse me, where's the canyon?'

This may be the most embarrassing question I have ever asked. I had been serving as a student leader at a camp for Navajo children in south-west Colorado. Since our return journey took us through Arizona, our bus took a detour so we could view one of the most spectacular places in God's creation, the Grand Canyon. The driver found the drop-off point, instructed us to return to that same spot in two hours, and drove off.

But there were no signs indicating where to go or what to do next. Apart from the road itself, all we could see were trees. Since I was a student leader, it fell to me to ask the dreaded question. I can still hear the snarky laugh of the park ranger as he pointed in the direction of the canyon. Why the laugh? It's because the Grand Canyon is more than a mile deep, as much as 18 miles wide, and 277 miles long! How could we miss something as vast as the Grand Canyon?

That's the question we ought to be asking about *inChristness*. It is the widest and deepest topic in the writings of the Apostle Paul. It is the Grand Canyon of his letters! And yet we almost never talk about it. Theologians do. They have to. Paul makes connections to this theme repeatedly. But the rest of us hardly ever think about it—much less talk about it—usually because we haven't been told where to find it, despite the fact that it is impossible to miss once you've been pointed in the right direction.

If you doubt that *inChristness* is so pervasive, I challenge you to start marking every time you see an expression like 'in Christ,' 'with Christ,' or 'through Christ' in the letters of Paul. You will encounter hundreds if you count everything connected to the theme. These expressions are so common that translators occasionally opt to leave out one or two because of Paul's tendency to pile them up.[2] Actually, Paul's generous use of such expressions can sometimes make them appear less important to us than they actually are. But maybe Paul wasn't mindlessly repeating *in-Christ* expressions at all. Perhaps he used repetition to emphasize the importance of living out the *in-Christ* life.

But what does it mean to be 'in' someone else—according to Paul? It means that you are so connected to the other that your life is no longer defined by you. It can be compared to a slave who not only gets released from slavery, but gets adopted. His new life is incorporated into the life of the one who adopted him and gets shaped by that new relationship (Gal. 4:7). It is like a woman whose life is so intertwined with her husband that their shared union defines her life (Rom. 7:2-4). It is like a prisoner who gets rescued from enemy territory and lives out the rest of his days in thankful service to the one who rescued him (Col. 1:12-14). It is like a soldier who is recruited by, fights alongside, suffers with, and lives only to please his commanding officer (2 Tim. 2:3-4).

Accordingly, let me suggest a definition: *InChristness*, or union with Christ, is being so connected to Christ that one's entire existence is defined by that connection. It includes how we got into a right relationship with God in the first place through Christ, what it means to share in Christ's death and resurrection, how we personally relate to Jesus, and how we are linked with other believers via our common association with Christ. Being *in Christ* is the Christian's identity. It is no exaggeration to claim that it is the most important thing about us.

Welcome to the in-Christ life. Your life is no longer your own. You are *in Christ*.

17

1

POSITION AND IDENTITY
IN CHRIST

CHAPTER 2

ACCESS TO GOD IN CHRIST

> 'Through him we have also obtained access by faith into this grace in which we stand, and we rejoice in hope of the glory of God' (Rom. 5:2).
>
> 'For through him we both have access in one Spirit to the Father' (Eph. 2:18).
>
> 'in whom we have boldness and access' (Eph. 3:12).

The line of cars backed up for miles. Trudi and I were desperately trying to get back into the Middle Eastern country we called home for seven years. But a border strike in a neighboring country obstructed our path. Fortunately, a conniving medical doctor convinced our bus driver to work his way to the front of the line, hoping for some sort of break. As our bus inched forward, the doctor interviewed everyone on board, searching out medical conditions that might get us through. Diabetes.... Asthma.... Headaches.... None of these would do. Then he spotted my wife. Eight months pregnant. Perfect!

The bus weaved its way to the front of the line. The doctor and driver disembarked with hopes that they might persuade two tea-sipping officials to allow our bus to cross the border. The doctor returned shortly, informing us that the officials wanted to see the pregnant woman. Trudi blissfully bounded off the bus. 'Slow down!' I hissed in English. So Trudi contorted her face, lumbered toward the officials, and drew labored breaths. When the border guards noticed her approach, they released a stream of expletives. An hour later, our bus was permitted to cross the border into our adopted country. We later learned that we were the only vehicle allowed passage for three whole days! We never would have received permission to pass apart from

Trudi. My wife gained access for us all. (The bus company refunded us the cost of our tickets out of gratitude.)

Our access to God is entirely because of Jesus. It isn't gained through anything we've accomplished. It is only because we are connected to Jesus that we have access to the Father.

There is more to this word 'access' in context than simply gaining entrée where none previously existed. When Romans 5:2 claims that through Christ we have obtained access to God, the implication is not only that we are given permission to enter God's presence, but also that we have One who personally introduces us as we come into God's presence, One who can justify doing so because He first justified us by grace through faith. That's why some translations render this rich word as 'introduction' rather than 'access.' We have access to God, to be sure, but we also have an introducer, Christ Jesus Himself. What if you were offered admission to the glorious throne room of the Almighty King of the Universe, but had to enter the hall alone? That would be terrifying! But Jesus, our Introducer, walks in front of us and introduces us—by name—to God the Father. It is through Christ that we have the right to come into God's presence.

I don't live overseas anymore. I now teach biblical studies at a Christian university. One of the most common complaints I hear from students is that they feel distant from God. There are many possible reasons they might feel this way, especially if their relationship with God is primarily based on their feelings. But before they can make any spiritual progress, they need to know that their access to God has been secured by Jesus. If they truly know Christ, their relationship with God is not broken, God is not distant, and Christ has not abandoned them. All of us who know Christ have been granted a relationship with God because of Christ's work on the cross. We can live in security and confidence that we have access to God *in Christ*.

CHAPTER 3

DEAD TO SIN IN CHRIST

> 'How can we who died to sin still live in it?' (Rom. 6:2)
>
> 'We know that our old self was crucified with him in order that the body of sin might be brought to nothing, so that we would no longer be enslaved to sin. For one who has died has been set free from sin' (Rom. 6:6-7).

'I feel like I'm in slavery. Is victory even possible?'

The student in my office had been describing a besetting sin. He had fought many battles to try to break free. Some he won; some he lost.

But repetitive sinning was not his destiny. If Paul could talk to him, Paul would explain that since this young man had died to sin, there was no reason to keep living in it. But, you know, Paul can sometimes be difficult to understand. Paul likes deep metaphors. Crucified with Christ is one of them. Dead to sin is another. Freedom from slavery is a third. All three show up in Romans 6.

Maybe we'll understand Paul's analogies better if we try one of our own. Bonded labor is one of the most common forms of slavery in the modern world. A desperately poor family seeks out the owner of a factory for help in paying medical bills. Forced labor is the means of paying off the contracted debt. But the terms and duration of such loans are often indefinite, resulting in long-term debt slavery.

I recently learned of a girl who was born in a brick kiln in Central Asia to parents who were bonded slaves. We'll call her Sara. Sara's father died when she was a baby. She grew up with her mother making one brick after another—all day long, seven days a week. Other children went to school; Sara made bricks. She was as much a slave as were the children of Israel who were forced to make bricks in Egypt. After the owner of the kiln murdered Sara's beloved mother, the teenaged orphan was coerced into a marriage contract with her 70-year-old master.

The day before the marriage was to take legal force, a pastor arrived with enough money to cover Sara's debt. Sara narrowly escaped with the pastor. She was free.

That day, Sara died to her old way of life. This doesn't mean that her former tormentor was dead, simply that his power over her was broken. To employ a common expression from the country where she resides, he had become 'dead to her.' His power was broken.

Freedom from the power of sin is one of the main points of Romans 6. We were all born in the kiln of sin. We were trapped in slavery. Apart from Christ, we remain slaves. In fact, captivity to sin constitutes a primary difference between an unbeliever and a believer. An unbeliever is in bondage to sin. It is impossible for an unbeliever not to sin. He can break an individual habit, but a related sin will pop up somewhere else in his life. He might get himself transferred from one room in the kiln to another, but he cannot escape his prison; he still has to obey sin, since sin is his taskmaster.

But if you truly know Christ, the power of sin is broken. You have walked out of the kiln with Christ. He paid your debt. You are free. There is more to say about overcoming sin than this, but here is where it all starts. To overcome sin you must first believe that Jesus has released you from the power of sin. A lot of young people I talk to don't actually believe this. They think they are stuck sinning and will never be able to break free. But the Bible declares that the power of sin has been broken because you are *in Christ.*

CHAPTER 4

ALIVE TO GOD IN CHRIST

> 'So you also must consider yourselves dead to sin and alive to God in Christ Jesus' (Rom. 6:11).

In the last chapter, I introduced you to Sara, a teenager who was rescued out of forced labor in a brick kiln in Central Asia. The day her debt was paid and she walked away from her slavery, Sara died to her old way of life. But what happened after that?

At the time of writing, Sara is seeking to build a new life. With the help of some foreign Christians, she has been able to buy a small home, purchase a sewing machine, and learn the rudimentary principles of the textile trade. A Christian woman has been helping Sara with remedial education, and, for the first time in her life, Sara is learning to read and write. This precious teenager has been enfolded into the life of a church where she is daily growing in her faith, learning the Scriptures, and worshiping God freely. Her dream is to one day become a teacher of the Bible.

Romans 6 proclaims that we have died to sin in Christ, but it also announces that we have risen with Christ to a new life. If a Hollywood studio decided to produce a film about Sara's life (highly unlikely), the movie would probably end at the moment Sara walked away from the brick kiln with the pastor. It would ignore what was required for her to build a new life. Come to think of it, if such a movie were produced in Hollywood, Sara probably wouldn't walk away with a pastor at all; she would narrowly escape with a muscular young man who single-handedly fought off a dozen armed guards to carry off his heart-throb in a helicopter!

But the film of our life isn't finished when we've been released from our slavery and the power of sin has been broken. In the truest of all senses, that's when the story starts. Like Sara, we entered a new life the moment we were rescued out of our own brick kiln. But as we build a new life in Christ, we must view ourselves as both dead to sin (the proper perspective on our past life) and alive to God in Christ Jesus (the proper perspective on our new life).

Sara undoubtedly will wake up some morning fearful that she is still enslaved in the depths of the brick kiln. It is not at all unlikely that the waves of desperation and shame Sara felt when she was a slave will still sometimes wash up on the shore of her heart. But whatever she feels inside, the objective truth is that Sara has been given a new life that was secured for her when her debt was paid. How tragic it would be if Sara were rescued from slavery, but ended up viewing herself with the same shame and desperation she felt when she was back in the kiln!

I know a young woman who lives like that. She cannot forgive herself for all the sins she committed in her past. She lives in constant awareness of the shame of those sins. She mentally accepts that Jesus paid her entire debt on the cross, but the memories of her past still have a hold on her.

Christian man or woman, hear me! *In Christ* you have entered a new life. One of the most important things you can do in your Christian life is to remember that Christ paid for all your sins so you could enter a new life filled with hope and love and fellowship with Him, and then live like all those things are true—which they are! Leave behind what you have left behind and live like one who is dead to sin and alive to God *in Christ*.

CHAPTER 5

NOT UNDER LAW THROUGH CHRIST

> 'Likewise, my brothers, you also have died to the law through the body of Christ, so that you may belong to another, to him who has been raised from the dead' (Rom. 7:4).
>
> 'For Christ is the end of the law for righteousness to everyone who believes' (Rom. 10:4).
>
> 'I do not nullify the grace of God, for if righteousness were through the law, then Christ died for no purpose' (Gal. 2:21).
>
> 'So then, the law was our guardian until Christ came, in order that we might be justified by faith. But now that faith has come, we are no longer under a guardian' (Gal. 3:24-25).

Is the goal of the Christian life to do your best to obey God's commands? What about the laws God gave to Israel through Moses? Is obedience to those laws the way to live a God-honoring life?

Let us acknowledge before proceeding that we can learn powerful truths about the holiness of God, the gravity of sin, and our need for atonement (among other biblical concepts) by paying careful attention to what is written in the Old Testament law. But as people *in Christ*, we now live under a different covenant than did the nation of Israel. Paul uses two illustrations from family life to make that point clear.

The first illustration compares the law to a wife who is bound by the covenant of marriage to stay married to her husband (Rom. 7:1-6). But after the death of her husband, she is free to remarry because the marriage covenant only applies until the death of a spouse.

The second illustration compares the law to a full-time babysitter (or 'guardian,' Gal. 3:24-25). After a child comes of age, there is no longer a need for the babysitter to oversee the activities of the child, because the child is now an adult.

Don't misunderstand. Paul views the Old Testament law as a good gift from God (Rom. 7:12). Paul views the law as good because it exposes our sin and shows us that we're sinners—which is a good thing—and because it leads to Christ—which is a very good thing (Rom. 3:20; 7:7; Gal. 3:24). But Paul is also clear that we are not to live life *under* the law (Rom 6:14; Gal. 5:18). Consequently, our orientation to life must not be moralistic, somehow thinking that if we just do the right things God's stamp of approval will be upon us. Just-follow-the-rules is not the way to live the life into which we were called. Rather, we need to stay focused on gospel truths: that we are in relationship with God only because Christ died in our place and offered us new life. In other words, we shouldn't view ourselves as law-keepers, but as those *in Christ*.

I know a professing Christian whose basic approach to life is simply one attempt after another to keep God's laws. What makes a critique of his lifestyle difficult is that much of what he does is good. He reads his Bible and prays. He doesn't commit adultery, intentionally lie, or try to cheat the government on his tax return. But his Christian life is as stale as a week-old loaf of bread. Why? One main reason is that his doctrine is off track. He thinks that somehow his moral rigor will make him look good in God's eyes. He needs to understand how the redemption of Christ has freed him from the mere obligation of law-keeping. He needs to start loving God and neighbor as he is filled with the love of Christ. And he needs to seek to act in ways that please God as overflow of thanksgiving for the grace he has received. But he'll only get there if he begins to view himself not as a law-keeper, but as one who is *in Christ*.

CHAPTER 6

NO CONDEMNATION IN CHRIST

> 'There is therefore now no condemnation for those who are in Christ Jesus' (Rom. 8:1).

'What's wrong with you?'

Someone quite close to me heard this harshly-intoned question hundreds of times during his childhood.

He heard it every time he made a mistake. 'What's wrong with you?' He heard it whenever he did something that made him stand out from other children. 'What's wrong with you?' He sometimes even heard it when he attempted to act in a kind or thoughtful way. 'What's wrong with you?' His dad, mom, and older sister all spoke these words frequently: 'What's wrong with you? What's wrong with you?'

It will come as no surprise that he grew up thinking that there was something wrong with him! But this is where it gets complicated. There really was something wrong with him. Not in the way you might think. Actually, measured on a human scale there was nothing wrong with him at all. He was exceptionally intelligent and unusually creative. But his creative endeavors made him appear different from the other members of his family, so they tried to coerce him to conform with words like: 'What's wrong with you?'

But, as I said, there actually was something wrong with him, even if the painful words he heard in his family missed the mark entirely. There is something wrong with me, as well. And I hope you'll allow that there is something wrong with you, too. We all inherited sin from Adam, and we personally choose to commit sins—lots of them. Whether our sin is the 'I'm going to do whatever I want' type, or the 'I'm better than everyone else' type, every person under heaven is a sinner, under condemnation, and deserving of God's punishment.

All of this has already been explained by the Apostle Paul in his magnificent letter to the Romans. In that letter, Paul has also explicated how Jesus's death on the cross was the means by which all who believe in Jesus are justified in God's sight. Furthermore, he has clarified that because of our connection to Christ we have died to sin and risen with Christ to a brand new life. Paul has even explained why the law has lost its jurisdiction over us. And he is just about to offer a breathtaking explanation of the role of the Holy Spirit in all of this. So when Paul cries out in the first verse of Romans 8, 'There is therefore now no condemnation for those who are in Christ Jesus!' he means it. Condemnation has been removed from those who are in Christ.

No condemnation. No more: 'What's wrong with you?' All that condemnation has been carried by Christ. So God doesn't condemn you. No condemnation! Others have no ground to condemn you. No condemnation! So you shouldn't condemn yourself either. No condemnation! Not even a little bit to make you feel like you've received some well-deserved pain for those sins you did despite knowing they were wrong. Not a hand slap, not a five-minute time out, not a disappointed expression on God's face. Jesus Himself bore all the condemnation on His own body; it is not yours to carry anymore.

So why are we still trying to carry it? Why do we keep listening to the condemning messages in our head? Maybe it's time to tell those thoughts to shut up—in Jesus's name! Over and over again. In place of the messages of condemnation, we can replace them with what we've encountered so far in this book—messages of transformation: 'I have access to God through Christ.' 'In Christ I have died to sin and have been raised to a new life.' 'I am united with Christ!' 'There is no condemnation *in Christ.*'

CHAPTER 7

CO-HEIRS WITH CHRIST

> 'and if children, then heirs—heirs of God and fellow heirs with Christ' (Rom. 8:17).
>
> 'So you are no longer a slave, but a son, and if a son, then an heir through God' (Gal. 4:7).
>
> 'In him we have obtained an inheritance' (Eph. 1:11).

If you were born in the State of Louisiana, you're luckier than you know. In the other 49 states of the USA, once you're an adult, your parents can disown you and cut you off from their inheritance for just about any reason. But in Louisiana, you can only be disinherited if your parents have 'just cause' (like you did something really, really bad to your parents). As for those of us who live in the other 49 states…well…too bad for the rest of us if our parents are so inclined.

Our spiritual inheritance is not based upon the whims of human parents, nor is it at risk as long as we haven't done something really, really bad, Louisiana-style. Our inheritance is grounded in *Christ*. We are co-heirs *with* Him; we have obtained our inheritance *in* Him. And that inheritance is so glorious, so splendid, and so limitless that there is plenty of it to go around. Sometimes when potential heirs enter probate court, they tussle and scuffle their way through lengthy litigation in an attempt to wrest from other potential heirs as fat a portion of the inheritance as possible. But the inheritance we will receive—sharing in the glory of Christ and ruling with Him in His future kingdom—is so vast that those on the receiving end won't be fretting that they didn't get enough of it. Besides, Christ Himself is our ultimate inheritance.

I once received a small inheritance. I inherited from my paternal grandmother one-thirtieth of a farm in Tennessee. A highly motivated relative whom I hardly knew figured out a way to get all the owners of the farm to sell the property at once. My portion of the income from the sale allowed me, an ex-missionary with no savings, to pay for graduate studies and a portion of my doctoral studies. I am deeply grateful that my grandmother was generous enough to include among her heirs not only her children, but her grandchildren as well.

But the only way I got a share in this inheritance was because I was *in* my dad. Apart from my connection to my dad, I never would have received that little plot of land in Tennessee. But I was connected to my dad, and my dad was connected to my grandmother. Similarly, the only way you or I will receive a portion of the inheritance that God is storing up for His children is through our connection to Jesus. Jesus has been named as the heir of a glorious future kingdom. We get to share in it, because we are receiving it *with* and *in* Him.

Included? Even in the inheritance? I am not just invited to dinner because someone noticed how sad my life was and felt sorry for me. I have been incorporated by grace into God's family, not as a housekeeper or a cook or a gardener, but as a dearly loved family member, sharing inheritance rights with Christ. The inheritance is still future, but the will and testament—with my name included as a designated heir—has already been drawn up, the signing has been witnessed, and the documents have been sealed by the Holy Spirit.

Brothers and sisters, let's look forward—longingly and with great hope—to the day we stand beside Christ in the presence of the Father and are presented a portion of the privileges that Christ by natural rights ought to inherit alone. We will receive this inheritance as co-heirs with Christ because our standing is *in Christ*.

CHAPTER 8

MEDIATION OF CHRIST

'Who is to condemn? Christ Jesus is the one who died—more than that, who was raised—who is at the right hand of God, who indeed is interceding for us' (Rom. 8:34).

'For there is one God, and there is one mediator between God and men, the man Christ Jesus' (1 Tim. 2:5).

One of the most important words in the Middle Eastern country where my wife and I lived for seven years is a word that literally means 'torpedo.' The way people on the streets use the term, though, has nothing to do with explosive devices; they use it to describe an important social phenomenon. It's a word everyone uses—all the time. Everyone needs this thing called 'torpedo.' It is basic to life in the Middle East.

When someone has 'torpedo,' he knows powerful people with influence who can help him get things accomplished. There is no English word that comes close to approximating this word in its context. The closest words I can think of are 'connections,' 'influence,' 'clout,' or 'contacts.'

The reason the word is so hard to translate is that in its Middle Eastern cultural context it is far more important than any of the English words I just suggested. Many people living in the Middle East tend toward fatalism: 'Whatever is going to happen is going to happen.' Unless, of course, you know people who have clout, that is, if you have 'torpedo.' If you don't have any 'torpedo,' life can be tough. Need a bank loan? No way…not without 'torpedo.' Your electricity got cut off and you're waiting for someone to fix it? You'll wait a long time without 'torpedo.'

Hoping for a favorable result at your upcoming trial? You need some 'torpedo,' and plenty of it.

The concept of 'torpedo' was just as important when Paul was writing letters as it is to people living in the Middle East today. Having access to a judge or to someone who knew the judge often was the difference in whether your court case got heard at all; and then if it did, whether you had a chance of receiving a favorable verdict. So when Paul wrote that Jesus sits in a place of honor at the right hand of God and intercedes on our behalf, this truth would have resonated deeply with Paul's readers. 'That's quite a connection! Who can condemn us? No one! Who can successfully bring a charge against God's elect? None, because our "torpedo" is with the One who intercedes for us before God—Christ Himself.'

Now only a few verses earlier in Romans 8, Paul said something similar about the Holy Spirit: that He intercedes for us when we pray. So both the Holy Spirit and Christ are said to intercede on our behalf, even though I think that Paul may have been viewing their respective intercessions in different ways. Paul may have been picturing the Holy Spirit (Rom. 8:26) more like a lawyer standing with his client and counseling him what to say; whereas Christ (Rom. 8:34) may be portrayed more like an advisor sitting next to a judge who also happens to personally know the defendant and can vouch for him. But Paul expands his second analogy almost to the bursting point when he intimates that the judge is the father of the one sitting next to him, and is willing to sacrifice the life of his own son for the sake of the defendant! This is cosmic 'torpedo' at its best!

Remember, if Christ didn't sit there next to the judge, your condemnation would be certain. It is only because Christ intercedes on your behalf that no charge can possibly stick. No wonder Paul breaks out in such exultant praise in the following verses! We have a mediator who intercedes for us, because we are *in Christ*.

CHAPTER 9

TRIUMPH THROUGH CHRIST

> 'No, in all these things we are more than conquerors through him who loved us' (Rom. 8:37).
>
> 'But thanks be to God, who gives us the victory through our Lord Jesus Christ' (1 Cor. 15:57).
>
> 'He disarmed the rulers and authorities and put them to open shame, by triumphing over them in him' (Col. 2:15).

Here's a paradox. How can Paul claim in Romans 8:37 that we are more than conquerors immediately after he mentions persecution, and just before he brings up demonic powers? Christians were persecuted in the first century, just as they are today. We don't always win. We face temptation and attack from Satan and his forces. We sometimes lose those battles. But Paul boldly proclaims, 'We are more than conquerors.' So are we victorious, or aren't we? Are we really conquerors?

Yes, we are…and no, we aren't—at least not yet. There is an already-ness to our lives in Christ and a not-yet-ness. Does it sound like I'm talking out of both sides of my mouth? Does this make any sense?

In truth, the only way to make any sense out of what the New Testament writers teach about the relationship of Christ's death to our daily lives is by affirming such statements as: 'It has happened now but isn't fully accomplished'; 'the kingdom has started but is not fully here'; 'the future has begun but is still coming.' There are many things in the New Testament we won't understand, including Paul's teaching about *inChristness,* unless we accept that such statements are necessary, and make every effort to wrap our lives around them.

Every year or two a rat will mount an attack on my property. This year a rat ate all my tomatoes before I knew it was in the neighborhood.

I hate rats. I view rats as being almost in the same category as demons. Intriguingly, rats have a tendency to show up during periods when I'm under spiritual attack. (There's no theological point to be made in this observation.) A couple of times rats have gotten into my garage and made a terrible mess.

The first time a rat made its way into my garage—before I had learned that setting rat traps was far smarter—I left a pack of poison under a shelf as a 'treat' for the rat. Now, this is where it gets nasty (feel free to skip to the end of the paragraph if you are a 'rat-aphobic'). The evil rat ate the poison and sealed his fate, but before that vermin died, it thrashed about, tore up linens, broke into food containers, left its feces all over the place (I warned you), and finally crawled into a corner to die. We discovered all this *after* we began to smell the decaying flesh of the repulsive creature. (Why did God create rats after all? Now *there's* a theological question I'd like answered!)

Jesus's death on the cross dealt Satan a mortal blow. That's why Paul can truthfully maintain that Jesus triumphed over Satan on the cross. But like our dying rat, Satan knows his destiny is assured and so he thrashes about in an attempt to destroy everything and everyone—up until his final moment. He is dangerous, far more dangerous than a dying rat—more like a wounded lion. But we can stand in confidence that his doom is sure. No maltreatment will ever be leveled against us that Christ hasn't provided a way through. No demon can mount an attack that will dislodge us from our entrenched position in Christ. We may encounter persecution and spiritual warfare, but we can know for certain that we share in Christ's victory—that we are more than conquerors—because our triumph is *in Christ*.

CHAPTER 10

NO SEPARATION IN CHRIST

'Who shall separate us from the love of Christ? Shall tribulation, or distress, or persecution, or famine, or nakedness, or danger, or sword?' (Rom. 8:35).

'For I am sure that neither death nor life, nor angels nor rulers, nor things present nor things to come, nor powers, nor height nor depth, nor anything else in all creation, will be able to separate us from the love of God in Christ Jesus our Lord' (Rom. 8:38-39).

We were half-way across the ocean, but tears still flowed freely. Trudi and I quietly wept in our airplane seats all the way across the continental United States and much of the way across the Atlantic Ocean as our plane hurtled us away from home toward Germany. Before boarding the plane, we exchanged tearful farewells with close family members at San Francisco International Airport. We didn't expect to see their faces again for years. Just before boarding the plane we sneaked one last backward look and couldn't help but notice the apprehension in our loved ones' eyes, that is, fear that they might never see us again.

But leaving family was only one part of the separation we encountered. Our new home was West Berlin. We arrived in that great city toward the end of the Cold War, one year before the Berlin Wall was dismantled. For eight months we resided in a building that was pocked with scars from the Second World War. Our neighborhood was packed full of Middle-Eastern guest workers. (We moved to Berlin to learn language among immigrants before moving to the Middle East.) We didn't know German, and we were just starting to learn the language of our target group. We arrived in Berlin in January when it was cold—

dark nights stretched out much longer than cloudy days. Berlin was a political island surrounded on all sides by eighty-seven miles of wall almost twelve feet high, behind which were stationed hundreds of East German and Russian military units. Not only were we separated from family, language, and good weather, in Berlin we were separated from the rest of the free world.

But regardless of our geography, we were *not* separated from the love of Christ, despite the intense loneliness and disorientation that greeted us every morning. God was with us, and we were still *in Christ.* We joined a ministry team consisting of three German women, a Korean family, a Dutch couple, and one American man—frequently gathering together with them for prayer. I discovered a walking path along a canal where I could pray; in the midst of human separation, I found solace in prayer. God ministered to Trudi through devotional books, worship music, and a Hayden trumpet concerto. Endless reminders of separation surrounded us, but we found ourselves progressively enveloped in the love of Christ. I wrote worship songs, and Trudi journaled. Nothing could separate us from our Lord. Nothing whatsoever could separate us from the love of Christ.

'But I don't always feel God's love.' I don't know how many times I have heard people say that. But before we start focusing on feelings, can we please make sure that we're first rooted in truth? In our last six chapters, we've taken some soundings in Romans 8. That glorious chapter starts with *No Condemnation* and ends with *No Separation.* In between, we learned about *No Loss of Inheritance* (Christ is co-heir), *No Judgment* (Christ mediates), and *No Defeat* (Christ triumphs). These are absolutely true—true truths!—whether we feel them or not. And although they are foundational to a changed life, they don't fluctuate like feelings do. Nothing at all—life, death, angels, demons, the present or the future—can separate us from the love of God in Christ Jesus our Lord. We participate in this truth and live in the reality of *No Separation* because we are *in Christ.*

CHAPTER 11

BELONGING TO CHRIST

> 'you are Christ's' (1 Cor. 3:23).
>
> 'If anyone is confident that he is Christ's, let him remind himself that just as he is Christ's, so also are we' (2 Cor. 10:7).
>
> 'those who belong to Christ Jesus' (Gal. 5:24).

Let me tell you something that may surprise you. Did you know that when a couple adopts a child in the United States, the government issues a brand new birth certificate for the child? The date of birth stays the same as what was on the old certificate, as does the hospital name and location. But the birth parents' names are new! When I first heard about this, it struck my historian ears as inappropriate. Who gave the government the right to alter history?

My wife and I adopted our two youngest daughters when they were eleven and almost nine respectively. According to their new certificates, Trudi gave birth to those girls, and I am their biological father. There is no documentary evidence that they were adopted. Anyone examining their two birth certificates would conclude that my wife had carried each daughter for nine months, hurried to the hospital when the labor pains started, and delivered those children from her own body. It's as though Trudi and I were actually there when they were born.

I may not like the idea that someone can alter history, but I do love the picture that emerges from this oddity of adoption law. When we were adopted into the family of God, Christ laid His claim on us. We are now His—and His completely. We don't belong to anyone else. All other claims have been revoked.

I recently heard about a woman who quit her job and moved from the East Coast to the West Coast of the United States to assist her older sister, the only relative with whom she had any connection. She made the move so she could care for her sister's children while her sister tried to recover from a debilitating illness. As it turned out, the health crisis persisted for more than a year, and the younger sister cared for the family through the entire time. But when the crisis was over, surprisingly and painfully, the older sister told the younger sister to leave. Sadly, the day she learned that she wasn't needed anymore, she learned that she wasn't really wanted either. This woman who had given up everything to serve her older sister was left without a job, a place to live, or a family.

Fortunately, she knew Christ. She located a church and got help from other believers. But she still struggles with the thought that she doesn't really belong anywhere or with anyone.

Similarly, some of the college students with whom I interact on a daily basis feel like they don't belong to anyone. At the beginning of each semester, I collect a personal bio from each student in every class I teach. I am regularly surprised by the response of many students to the simplest of all questions on the information sheet: Where are you from? Where do you call home? Some students are only able to reply to this question with the name of their dorm. They may have grown up somewhere else, but they don't feel like they belong there.

Dear Christian brother or sister, do you feel this way? Does it seem like you don't belong in any place or in any group or even in any family? Let me tell you by the authority of the Word of God that if you are a child of God, you belong to Christ. He exclaims, 'You are mine! You are my beloved! You belong here right next to me!'

You belong to Christ, dear friend, because you are *in Christ*.

CHAPTER 12

JUSTIFIED IN CHRIST

> 'And such were some of you. But you were washed, you were sanctified, you were justified in the name of the Lord Jesus Christ and by the Spirit of our God' (1 Cor. 6:11).
>
> 'But when the goodness and loving kindness of God our Savior appeared, he saved us, not because of works done by us in righteousness, but according to his own mercy, by the washing of regeneration and renewal of the Holy Spirit, whom he poured out on us richly through Jesus Christ our Savior, so that being justified by his grace we might become heirs according to the hope of eternal life' (Titus 3:4-7).

Diplomatic immunity. That's what we all wish we had whenever we get pulled over for speeding. Imagine being able to say, 'I'm sorry, Mr. Policeman, you can't give me a ticket. I have *diplomatic immunity.*' Or suppose you found yourself in the presence of a judge who demanded immediate payment for the 25,000 parking tickets you had knowingly ignored. Wouldn't it be great to be able to say, 'I'm sorry, Mrs. Judge, I don't have to pay for those tickets. I have *diplomatic immunity.*'

Justification is something like diplomatic legal immunity. Justification has nothing to do with looking for a way to justify our actions—as though we really didn't do anything wrong in the first place. The opposite is the case. Biblical justification is receiving legal acquittal *despite* our serious and repeated sins. That may be why Paul rehearses some past sins of the Corinthians just before he brings up justification in 1 Corinthians 6:11: sexual immorality, idolatry, greed, drunkenness, fighting, and swindling (6:9-10). It is with such sins underscored—not ignored—that Paul reminds the Corinthians that they were washed, sanctified, and justified (each a unique picture of salvation) in the name of Jesus (6:11).

In a different passage about justification to his mentee Titus, Paul announces that it is 'not because of works done by us in righteousness' that we are saved, but simply because we are 'justified by his grace' (Titus 3:4-7). Even if someone were somehow to live a really, *really* good life, and only commit one little sin a day for 70 years, he would still rack up 25,000 sins by the end of his life.[3] No one gets off the hook for even one sin, much less 25,000 sins—even if they are only parking tickets—unless, of course, you have been granted diplomatic immunity.

That is something like our standing before God if we have been saved 'through Jesus Christ our Savior' (Titus 3:6). We have been justified despite all our sins. We can claim *in-Christ immunity*. Just as a diplomat cannot be prosecuted in a foreign country regardless of whether his past record includes 25,000 parking tickets, neither will God the judge hold us accountable for our sins when we enter His country. Why? It is only because we have been justified—granted the most comprehensive immunity possible—'in the name of the Lord Jesus Christ' (1 Cor. 6:11) that we are free from prosecution both for our 'small' infractions as well as our serious crimes. Just as a diplomat's standing is based upon his connection to an entity outside of himself, so also on the basis of our connection to Jesus Christ—and based upon that connection alone—we are exempt from prosecution for our sins.

God has declared us justified in His sight. If God has declared it so—and has moved heaven and earth to make it so—who are we to live like it isn't so? We can claim the confidence of a new standing in Christ. We will never be tried and convicted for our sins if we have been united with Christ. We have a changed standing because we belong to Christ. We have been justified *in Christ.*

CHAPTER 13

SLAVES BUT FREE IN CHRIST

> 'For he who was called in the Lord as a bondservant is a freedman of the Lord. Likewise he who was free when called is a bondservant of Christ. You were bought with a price' (1 Cor. 7:22-23).

You are not defined by obligation. Neither are you defined by freedom from obligation. You are defined by your *inChristness*. Suppose that your father and mother were both slaves, and as a consequence you were born into slavery. As a believer in Jesus, you shouldn't view yourself as a slave; you should view yourself as one Christ has set free. Were you born free? Then you need to change your perspective, too. As someone *in Christ* you should start regarding yourself as a slave of Christ.

German Moravian missionaries Johann Leonhard Dober and David Nitschmann left Germany in 1732 intent on reaching out in Christian love and gospel proclamation to African slaves on the islands of St. Croix and St. Thomas in the Caribbean. When the two men traveled to Denmark to try to procure passage to the islands, their intentions became known to personnel of the Danish West India Company, who strongly opposed them. But the two persisted, to the point of offering to *become slaves themselves* so they could reach the slaves. This offer, apparently, was refused, so the men appealed directly to and received permission from the queen of Denmark to pursue their mission. The owners of the Danish West India Company continued to oppose the missionaries and wouldn't allow passage on any of their ships, but Dober and Nitschmann found a roundabout way to the islands anyway. There they plied their trades, lived simply, and reached out as they were able to those unjustly enslaved.[4]

These two men, and the other Moravians who followed in their footsteps, taught the converted slaves to view themselves as the Lord's freedpersons, even while Dober and Nitschmann viewed themselves as the Lord's slaves—as seen in their willingness to become actual slaves. They lived out their service to their heavenly Master, knowing that they belonged to Him. Most of us need to learn *both* truths—that we are at the same time the Lord's slaves and the Lord's freedpersons. While it may be the case that a slave on earth especially needs to learn that in Christ he is free, and a person born free needs to learn about living as a slave of Christ, almost everyone can be helped by internalizing both concepts.

Without minimizing the harsh realities of physical slavery, it is still true that while most people in the world are not legal slaves, many are not free to pursue the things they want. Multitudes of people work menial jobs that seem to lead nowhere, but are unable to quit because their families depend upon their income. Others are trying to pay off school or medical debts, and are thereby forced to live meager existences. Still others spend their days caring for multiple young children in small houses or apartments where they feel trapped. All of them can find freedom of heart in learning the truth that they are indeed freedpersons in Christ!

It may be, however, that you grew up with a certain amount of privilege. Possessions and opportunities have been given to you. The primary pressure you feel is struggling to choose between multiple good options. In your case, the crucial truth to learn may be that you are a slave of Christ; your life is no longer your own. 'You were bought with a price,' says Paul in 1 Corinthians 7:23, which means that now you belong to someone else.

Most of us need to internalize both truths, since both are in fact true, and both are important. You are a slave, and you are a freedperson—a slave *of Christ* and a freedperson *in Christ*.

CHAPTER 14

FUTURE RESURRECTION IN CHRIST

'But in fact Christ has been raised from the dead, the firstfruits of those who have fallen asleep. For as by a man came death, by a man has come also the resurrection of the dead. For as in Adam all die, so also in Christ shall all be made alive' (1 Cor. 15:20-22).

'knowing that he who raised the Lord Jesus will raise us also with Jesus and bring us with you into his presence' (2 Cor. 4:14).

'For since we believe that Jesus died and rose again, even so, through Jesus, God will bring with him those who have fallen asleep' (1 Thess. 4:14).

Do you remember reading about the Greek philosopher Plato in high school? Did you know that Plato sometimes comes to church with us? That is, Christians often unknowingly carry around with them some of Plato's ideas about spirits and bodies. Plato was a brilliant man who advanced all sorts of helpful thoughts, but one less-than-helpful idea he promoted—and that has come to dominate many Christians' view of heaven—is that non-material things like ideas or spiritual realities are basically good, whereas physical things like human bodies are basically evil. Some Christians after the time of the apostles were influenced by the ideas of Plato on this subject, with the result that many Christians throughout history—and today as well—have come to believe that the heaven they will one day inhabit is an ethereal place where spirits float around in endless tranquility apart from their bodies. Thus the image of sitting on clouds surrounded by never-ending white-ness...

Do *you* want to live a disembodied existence like that? I didn't think so! Neither do I. Fortunately, that's not what the Bible teaches about the New Heavens and the New Earth. But how do we know that this isn't what Scripture teaches? We know primarily because Jesus Christ took on human flesh, was crucified in a human body, and was resurrected *in a body*! Since we have been united with Him—that is, since we are *in Him*—our resurrection will be like His resurrection! Our resurrected bodies will be like His (Phil. 3:20-21).

This means that our long-term future will be both spiritual *and* physical. Many of the things that we love about the current physical world foreshadow good things that we will get to share in the future. Do you love good food? There will be wonderful food to enjoy in the place Jesus is preparing. Do you enjoy sitting beside a river under the shade of a lush tree? Take a look at Revelation 21–22 (esp. 22:1-5) and pay attention to the details. Does the place described there sound like a description of floating on endless white clouds?

Consequently, when you enjoy a wonderful meal, consider it a foretaste of even-better food you will one day enjoy in a resurrected body—and allow the tastes to create an anticipation of even richer tastes that you will experience after the resurrection. As you wrap up a spiritually encouraging conversation with a godly person, let the encouragement you feel at the end of that conversation function as a preview of many more encouraging conversations you will have in the future, including with the great saints of the past. When you sense consolation and comfort from the Lord after a time of prayer under a lush tree beside a river, let that moment spark in you an expectation for future conversations with the Lord Jesus Himself, who may even sit beside you under the tree of life and converse with you! There is much more besides what I have mentioned to look forward to in the future if you are united with Christ by faith. In light of the future resurrection that awaits you, aren't you thankful to be *in Christ*?

CHAPTER 15

VEIL REMOVED IN CHRIST

'Since we have such a hope, we are very bold, not like Moses, who would put a veil over his face so that the Israelites might not gaze at the outcome of what was being brought to an end. But their minds were hardened. For to this day, when they read the old covenant, that same veil remains unlifted, because only through Christ is it taken away. Yes, to this day whenever Moses is read a veil lies over their hearts. But when one turns to the Lord, the veil is removed' (2 Cor. 3:12-16).

In his short classic, *Animal Farm*, George Orwell spins an engaging tale of farm animals who stage a revolt.[5] After driving away their human masters, the pigs—the smartest of the beasts—organize the first-ever animal-governed farm. Unfortunately, the animals' desire to create a utopian society free of human influence gets undermined by the power-grab of the pigs, and of one pompous pig in particular.

But *Animal Farm* is not a fairy tale about animals; it is political satire directed toward communist Russia under the dictatorship of Joseph Stalin. This is *key* to understanding Orwell's book. Anyone who reads *Animal Farm* without utilizing this overall interpretive key is like someone who tries to read a book through a thick veil. They have a surface-level understanding, but are missing the author's primary intention.

In 2 Corinthians 3:12-16 Paul tells us that the key to understanding the Old Testament, including the law of Moses, is *Christ*. Those who don't accept that the law of Moses ultimately points to Jesus are hopelessly trying to understand the message of Moses as though gazing at him through a thick veil. All who reject Jesus—and Paul was thinking of so many of his fellow Jews who did not accept Jesus—are like the congregation of Israel who gazed at Moses while he was wearing a veil, and so could not understand the primary purpose of his instructions because 'their minds were hardened.' So instead of accepting that God's primary purpose in giving the Law—indeed, in giving the entire Old Covenant—was to point people toward Jesus, those who gaze through a veil often ended up focusing on the *laws* themselves. Those who read the words of Moses through a veil couldn't—and can't today—see the big picture of the Bible. Furthermore, 'to this day, when they read the old covenant, that same veil remains unlifted.'

'But,' writes Paul, 'when one turns to the Lord, the veil is removed.' The basis for removing this veil of misunderstanding is *inChristness*. Paul declares that 'only through Christ is it taken away.'

Does this mean that every time an unbeliever interprets a Bible verse he gets it wrong? No. Unbelievers too can understand the meaning of a given Bible verse if they pay careful attention to its context. But unless they personally embrace and commit themselves to the truth that the Bible's central message is Jesus, including the old covenant laws given through Moses, they will still miss the *main thing*—the essential point of the Bible. Just as someone is bound to misunderstand *Animal Farm* if he stubbornly insists on reading it as a fairy tale about animals, someone who doesn't personally embrace Jesus as Messiah will struggle to accept that the Bible is anything more than a collection of disconnected stories, letters, laws, and poetry.

This means that understanding what the Bible is all about is inextricably connected to *inChristness*. Do you want to be someone who understands the Bible? You will only grasp the Main Thing about the Bible when you embrace the Main Person of the Bible; otherwise, the main concerns of the Bible will be veiled to you. The veil of misunderstanding is removed *in Christ.*

CHAPTER 16

A NEW CREATION IN CHRIST

> 'Therefore, if anyone is in Christ, he is a new creation. The old has passed away; behold, the new has come' (2 Cor. 5:17).

Authenticity. Now there's an important word in our generation. Young people are fed up with fakeness and sick of sham. Not long ago a youth pastor told me that the kids in his youth group preferred listening to unpolished or even stammering speakers whom they perceived as genuine over speakers who were slick but inauthentic. Young people today are crying out for authenticity.

But I'm afraid that an irony often accompanies this quest for authenticity. Many of the same young people who place such a high value on authenticity daily present themselves on social media as funny, witty, independent, caring, or cool—when in real life they may be none of those. Those who shout loudest for authenticity in others often fake it themselves.

Honestly, I've recently grown to dislike the word *authenticity* because of the way the word has come to be used in contemporary discourse. Many of the young people I talk to view authenticity as acting in line with one's feelings. They have been led to believe that they will only find meaning in life by discovering their own personal reality (that may, in fact, have little connection to real reality) and then live according to *that.* The quest to construct a personal reality and openly proclaim it is viewed as authenticity.

But real authenticity—authentic authenticity, if you will—cannot be based upon the way you feel; otherwise, what will happen when you start feeling something different tomorrow? A biblically-rooted authenticity must center on living according to what is *true*—about God and about what God has done in and for you through Christ.

So what is true? 'Therefore, if anyone is in Christ, he is a new creation. The old has passed away; behold, the new has come' (2 Cor. 5:17). As someone in Christ, your *real reality*, your *true truth* is something you didn't make up. If you have bought the lie that you need to construct a personal reality—that you are the maker of meaning and the source of your significance—then you have sold your birthright for a pot of porridge.

God declares that you are *a new creation* because of your connection to Jesus! This means that you must learn how to live according to that new reality. Do you long for an authentic life, a life that agrees with what God says about you? A biblically-authentic Christian affirms new life in Christ. A biblically-authentic Christian focuses on the truth that the old way of life has passed and a new reality has replaced it. A biblically-authentic Christian rejects false identities and personally-constructed 'realities.' A biblically-authentic Christian lives like he or she is *in Christ.*

In its context, the declaration that the old has passed and the new has come means that the standard by which we evaluate people, including ourselves, is no longer human or worldly (literally in Greek, no longer *according to the flesh*, 2 Cor. 5:16). So, even though we used to live for ourselves, we don't live that way any longer; we live solely and completely for Christ (2 Cor. 5:15).

I'm thinking of someone whose past is dreadful. The sheer number and intensity of hurts she has experienced in her relatively short life are unspeakable. But this lovely young woman has decided not to live according to her past. She has grounded herself in what the Bible says about her new life. She believes that she is in Christ, that the old has passed, and that the new has come. Now *that's* an authentic life.

A truly authentic life is not dependent upon one's feelings, but is lived in accord with the truth that we are new creations *in Christ.*

CHAPTER 17

IDENTITY IN CHRIST

> 'I know a man in Christ' (2 Cor. 12:2).
>
> 'those who are in Christ Jesus' (Rom. 8:1).
>
> 'they were in Christ before me' (Rom. 16:7).
>
> 'And because of him you are in Christ Jesus' (1 Cor. 1:30).
>
> 'if anyone is in Christ' (2 Cor. 5:17).
>
> 'Greet every saint in Christ Jesus' (Phil. 4:21).
>
> 'To the saints and faithful brothers in Christ' (Col. 1:2).

The proconsul was insistent, and said, 'Swear the oath and I will let you go! Revile Christ!'

Polycarp replied, 'Eighty–six years I have served him, and he has never wronged me. How can I blaspheme my King who saved me?'

But the proconsul continued to insist, saying, 'Swear by the genius of Caesar!'

So Polycarp replied, 'If you vainly expect that I will swear by the genius of Caesar, as you say, and pretend that you do not know who I am, then listen carefully: I am a Christian.'[6]

The speaker, Polycarp of Smyrna, was probably the most influential Christian in the earliest decades after the passing of the apostles. He has also been an important influence in my life. I've lived in the city in western Asia where he lived. My oldest daughter was born there. I've written academic articles about him, a doctoral dissertation on the literary relationship of Polycarp and Paul, and a narrative introduction to the Apostolic Fathers in which he is the primary teacher.[7] After the Apostle Paul, Polycarp is my most important historical mentor. (Jesus is not my mentor; He is my *Lord!*)

Polycarp was executed by a Roman proconsul because he would not waver in holding to his identity as a Christian. If ever there was someone who had a clear understanding of his identity, it was Polycarp. When the proconsul tried to pressure Polycarp to renounce his faith, the elderly Polycarp addressed him slowly and deliberately, *'If you… pretend that you do not know who I am, then listen carefully: I am a Christian.'* He was publicly burned because he knew who he was and refused to back down from it.

My other historical mentor, Paul, never used the word 'Christian' in all of his writings. If that seems strange to you, remember that the term 'Christian' was just starting to be used when Paul wrote his letters (Acts 11:26). So instead of employing the word 'Christian,' Paul often just labeled disciples as those who were *in Christ*. He didn't need a different label, of course, since the most important thing about Christ-followers is their *inChristness*.

During one debate leading up to an American presidential election, I once heard an isolationist-leaning candidate make the following (ominous) statement: 'If we don't know who you are when you arrive at our borders, you're not getting into our country.'[8] When I heard this comment, I found myself asking: What does he mean by 'knowing who you are'? It must mean knowing your background…maybe where you have lived, where you have worked; but it most certainly means *who you are connected to*.

This candidate at least got one part right: the central issue in your identity is who you are connected to. Some people are connected to upright citizens; others to subversive groups. If you are a Christian, your most important connection is to Christ.

Suppose that an immigration officer—or worse, a Roman proconsul intent on halting the spread of Christianity—was trying to determine who you are. Would it be obvious that your primary connection is to Christ?

Polycarp got it right. The most important thing about our identity is that we are Christians. Paul would have agreed, but he wouldn't have called us Christians. He would have said that we are *in Christ*.

CHAPTER 18

CHRIST IN US

> 'Or do you not realize this about yourselves, that Jesus Christ is in you?' (2 Cor. 13:5)
>
> 'It is no longer I who live, but Christ who lives in me' (Gal. 2:20).
>
> 'so that Christ may dwell in your hearts through faith' (Eph. 3:17).
>
> 'Christ in you, the hope of glory' (Col. 1:27).

Our focus in this book is on *inChristness*. That's because the Apostle Paul repeatedly and insistently emphasized that we are *in Christ*—not to mention the fact that we rarely talk about it in our churches. But Paul also occasionally wrote about Christ living *in us*. It is surprising to me, especially when we consider Paul's emphases, that Christians today are far more familiar with the concept of Christ being in us than they are with what it means to live in Christ.

The rest of this book focuses on *inChristness;* but in this chapter I want to reflect on the rich concept of *Christ-in-us*, which is a companion teaching to *inChristness* in the letters of Paul.

Christ lives in us. How can this be? It turns out that Jesus anticipated that His disciples might eventually wonder about this. So, in advance, He told His disciples that He was going away (John 13:33; 14:2). But He also said that He would come to them (John 14:3, 28). How can both be possible? Both are possible because God sent the Spirit, who sometimes in the Bible is called 'the Spirit of Christ' (John 14:16-18).

When we come to Paul's letters, we discover that *indwelling* is more commonly associated with the Holy Spirit than with Christ (1 Cor. 6:19; 2 Tim. 1:14). But because Jesus is fully God and the Holy Spirit is fully God, the Apostle Paul didn't hesitate to say in one breath, 'the

Spirit of God dwells in you,' and in the very next breath 'Christ is in you' (Rom. 8:9-10). Through the indwelling of the Holy Spirit, Christ is present in everyone who believes.

So, Christ is in us through His Spirit. What difference does it make? Robert Munger creatively brought home the truth of the indwelling of Christ in his poignant little allegory, *My Heart – Christ's Home.*[9] After inviting Christ into his home (that is, his life) he took the Lord into the rooms of his house one-by-one and permitted him to clean out whatever didn't belong there. In the first room, the Study, Christ helped him redirect his reading priorities, so he began to spend more time in the Bible. In the Dining Room, Christ helped him identify and correct his misplaced pleasures and appetites. In the Living Room, Christ led him into discovering the richness of fellowship and friendship with his Lord. In the Workroom, Christ equipped him for kingdom work. In the Rec Room, Christ helped him think through how to include the Lord in his recreational activities and relationships. The narrator even eventually allowed Christ to clean out the tiny upstairs closet that contained a few secret stashes that were starting to rot. In the end, the narrator came to realize that he was still treating Christ as a guest in his house instead of as its master, so he entirely relinquished ownership and transferred the title. The final sentence of the allegory reads: 'Things are different since Jesus Christ has settled down and has made His home in my heart.'

Paul prayed for his readers 'that Christ may dwell in your hearts through faith' (Eph. 3:17). I'm pretty sure that he didn't want us to leave Jesus standing in the front hall. Paul was praying that we would give over the master key to every room in our house, relinquish the deed, and acknowledge that Jesus is the actual owner of the entire house.

So it turns out that union with Christ goes both ways: We are *in Christ*, and Christ is *in us*.

CHAPTER 19

SUBSTITUTION OF CHRIST

'who gave himself for our sins' (Gal. 1:4).

'For our sake he made him to be sin who knew no sin, so that in him we might become the righteousness of God' (2 Cor. 5:21).

'whom God put forward as a propitiation by his blood' (Rom. 3:25).

'For while we were still weak, at the right time Christ died for the ungodly. For one will scarcely die for a righteous person—though perhaps for a good person one would dare even to die—but God shows his love for us in that while we were still sinners, Christ died for us' (Rom. 5:6-8).

Jesus died in our place. The death that we deserved, He died instead. The punishment that should have fallen on us fell upon Him instead.

In 1925, Turkish storyteller Ömer Seyfettin wrote a story entitled *The Oath*, a well-known story in Turkey to this day. In the story Seyfettin writes of Ahmet Aslan and his childhood friend Mistik. Ahmet was twelve years old when he and Mistik solemnly promised their allegiance to each other. They sealed their commitment with a ritual of blood—the details of which you probably don't want to read.

Only a few weeks after they made their pledge they were coming out of school and heard some men shouting. Suddenly, a crazed dog sprinted straight toward them being chased by three men. 'Run! The dog is dangerous!'

The two boys tried to escape, but Ahmet tripped and fell. The dog rushed toward him. Ahmet cried out.

Mistik heard his friend's shout, turned and headed back toward him. At the last second, instead of attacking Ahmet, the dog jumped over Ahmet and lunged at Mistik, knocking him to the ground and biting him ferociously. The three men ran as quickly as they could, beat the vicious dog off Mistik with sticks, and drove it away. Mistik tried to stand up, but was hurt and bleeding. One of the men spoke insistently to the boy, 'We need to take you straight home. That dog was sick.'

The next day Mistik wasn't at school. Ahmet wanted to know how he was doing. But Mistik's mom wouldn't let him see his friend. 'He is sick...very sick.'

The following day Ahmet learned that Mistik had been transferred to a hospital in Istanbul. The boy decided to stop by Mistik's house after school to see if he could learn anything more about his friend. Mistik's mother opened the front door, her eyes bloodshot. When Ahmet asked about Mistik, her eyes filled with tears and she spoke in a whisper. 'Mistik passed away last night. Mistik is...dead.'

She cried. Ahmet cried with her. His brother—his blood brother—was dead.

The story ends imagining an elderly Ahmet reflecting back on the day he fell when trying to flee from the dog. 'I'm an old man now. Many years have passed, but I remember it all as if it happened yesterday. Whenever I look at the scar on my finger from the time we made our promise in blood, I think of my friend Mistik who died in my place. It should have been me. I should have been the one who died. But I'm alive because of my blood brother who gave his life for me.' [10]

Jesus is our true blood brother who took upon Himself the fury that should have been directed toward us. He did it for you; He did it for me—and for all who are *in Christ*.

CHAPTER 20

PROMISES IN CHRIST

'so that in Christ Jesus the blessing of Abraham might come to the Gentiles' (Gal. 3:14).

'so that the promise by faith in Jesus Christ might be given to those who believe' (Gal. 3:22).

'As surely as God is faithful, our word to you has not been Yes and No. For the Son of God, Jesus Christ, whom we proclaimed among you, Silvanus and Timothy and I, was not Yes and No, but in him it is always Yes. For all the promises of God find their Yes in him. That is why it is through him that we utter our Amen to God for his glory' (2 Cor. 1:18-20).

She broke her promise. She vowed to love, respect, and stay faithful to her husband—for better or worse, for richer or poorer, in sickness and health, till death parted them. But she was enticed by an immoral man, and after the first, others like him. Her unfaithfulness became a habit, and her habit a lifestyle. Her husband pleaded with her, ardently sought to draw her back, and reminded her of her vows. More importantly, he reminded her of *his* vows, vows to be faithful, vows that he would never violate, no matter what.

This story is true. It gets rehearsed again and again by the prophets of Israel and Judah as they compare God's covenant-people with a woman who broke her vows despite the relentless fidelity of her husband (e.g., Hosea 2; Ezek. 16).

God is a God who keeps His promises. Promise-keeping is one of the most important themes in the Bible. God makes a promise and God keeps that promise. In fact, this theme is so prominent that one way to organize the entire Bible is around the theme of promise-keeping.

Solemn promises in the Bible are referred to as covenants. Ponder for a moment what it means for the Creator of the Universe to bind Himself to a covenant. When God enters into a covenant, what He promises to do becomes an inviolable oath because it is guaranteed by His own unchangeable character and His inability to lie. Now, there were smaller covenants 'cut' in the Old Testament (that is how covenant-making is described in Hebrew), but God cut major covenants during the lifetimes of Noah, Abraham, Moses, and David. And then He promised that in the future He would cut an even better covenant, a New Covenant (Jer. 31:31-34). The New Testament is insistent that all these covenants find their ultimate fulfillment in the person and work of Jesus.

For a Christian, the fact that God has been and continues to be faithful to His promises impacts many areas of life, both large and small. For example, in 2 Corinthians 1:18-20, we encounter the Apostle Paul reacting to the accusation that he wavered in his intention to visit the Corinthians. 'Was I vacillating…? Do I make my plans according to the flesh, ready to say "Yes, yes" and "No, no" at the same time?' (2 Cor. 1:17). His response: Absolutely not…and let me tell you why. The God who is faithful to keep His promises has fulfilled all the promises He made *in Christ* (1:18-20). Paul puts it powerfully: 'in him it is always Yes. For all the promises of God find their Yes in him.'

Yes! *In Christ* we have been bound to this covenant-keeping God! So if we make a God-honoring promise and keep it—whether to complete a promised task, or to spend more time with our children, or to remain faithful to the spouse of our young adulthood, or to follow Christ— we broadcast to those around us something about the character of a God who fulfilled all His covenants by sending Christ. We get to share in God's promise-keeping agenda, since all the promises of God are fulfilled *in Christ*.

CHAPTER 21

BAPTIZED INTO CHRIST

'For as many of you as were baptized into Christ' (Gal. 3:27).

'having been buried with him in baptism, in which you were also raised with him through faith in the powerful working of God, who raised him from the dead' (Col. 2:12).

'Do you not know that all of us who have been baptized into Christ Jesus were baptized into his death? We were buried therefore with him by baptism into death, in order that, just as Christ was raised from the dead by the glory of the Father, we too might walk in newness of life' (Rom. 6:3-4).

Four people were baptized 'into Christ Jesus' this week at the church where I worship. This is a common occurrence at my church. Baptism is a time when young and old publicly declare their faith in Jesus Christ. I love baptisms, and I love the accompanying testimonies of those who are baptized.

Baptism in the Bible, however, carries a few surprising associations. First, the Apostle Paul spiritually compares baptism to dying with Christ (taken down into the water), being buried with Christ (put under the water), and rising with Christ (taken up from the water). That is, in fact, the basic meaning of baptism. Most of us know that. But the burial part, actually, is a bit surprising when you stop to think about it. Focusing on the death and resurrection of Christ makes perfect sense, since Christ's death and resurrection are the center-point of the Christian faith. But why include burial as part of the baptismal pattern (e.g., 1 Cor. 15:4;

Col. 2:12; Rom. 6:4)? Short answer: Burial emphasizes the *finality* of death to our old way of life. Mentioning burial reminds us of that.

Another surprise is that the Greek word for 'baptize' in Greek literature outside the New Testament often describes a cataclysmic event rather than something warm and fuzzy. People who drown in the sea are described as being baptized. Even sunken ships are referred to as 'baptized.' Mobs who overrun and trash a city 'baptize' the place.[11] The point is that the use of this word in the Bible to describe our break from our old life of sin points to how it should be *decisive*.

Another surprising thing is that a couple of times in the Bible the word 'baptism' is used all by itself when referring to salvation. Now, I want to be absolutely clear about this. Water baptism does *not* save you. Paul spends way too much time arguing that salvation is by grace through faith to allow for that (Rom. 5:2; Eph. 2:8-9). But baptism symbolizes the breaking with our old lives (repentance) and entering into a new life (faith), and so functions as a simple shorthand way of describing the process. That's why Paul can sometimes describe salvation simply as being 'baptized into Christ' (Gal. 3:27).

The most surprising thing of all about baptism is that *we* are said to share somehow in Jesus's death, burial, and resurrection. But how can we share in a once-in-eternity event—the most important event in history? Let us acknowledge that the death-burial-resurrection event is uniquely Christ's. Christ Jesus alone carried the guilt of humankind on His body on the cross. He alone took the punishment that was deservedly ours. That's what makes it so surprising that He would share His death, burial, and resurrection with us in any way at all. But the Bible teaches that somehow He did (Col. 2:12; Rom. 6:3-4). What this likely means is that when we believed, we became associated with Christ to such a degree that what transpired can be compared to death, burial, and resurrection. Praise God that our lives are now so closely identified with Jesus, that we can view our spiritual baptism as death to our life of sin and being raised to a new life *in Christ*.

CHAPTER 22

CLOTHED WITH CHRIST

> 'For as many of you as were baptized into Christ have put on Christ' (Gal. 3:27).
>
> 'So then let us cast off the works of darkness and put on the armor of light...put on the Lord Jesus Christ, and make no provision for the flesh, to gratify its desires' (Rom. 13:12b, 14).

For many years, for reasons unknown to me, all four of my teenaged and young adult daughters asked me to pass on my old shirts to them when I was ready to dispense with them, especially my comfortable long-sleeved flannel ones. My daughters vied with one another to see who could get the next shirt I was ready to discard! Honestly, I couldn't understand it when I would spy one of my beautiful daughters heading down the hall on her way to bed wearing one of my worn out (though much loved!) shirts—shirts that were too long and too wide for them, and not a bit in style.

I recently asked my daughters why (in the world!) they would want my old shirts. I'd never directly asked them, and so continued to be mystified by their strange requests. But each daughter in her own way communicated that wearing my old shirts made her feel (1) secure and (2) comforted.

The Apostle Paul explains that when we were baptized into Christ (that is, saved), we put on Christ like putting on a garment (Gal. 3:27). In a different passage and context, Paul tells us that if we don't want to give in to our fleshly desires, we need to clothe ourselves with Christ (Rom. 13:14). The first of these two passages (Gal. 3:27) focuses upon our standing in Christ. We believed the gospel of Christ and are now wrapped in the righteousness of Christ. We are dressed in His righteousness, so that when God looks at us, He sees Christ. The second of these passages (Rom. 13:14) helps us live out this truth in daily life. One helpful way of thinking about the relationship between these two passages is that we shouldn't allow the garment with which we have been clothed (Christ Himself) to hang loose. We need to pull Christ close and hold Him tight.

Security and comfort. These were the reasons my daughters told me they wanted my old shirts. Similarly, we are secure because we have been clothed with Christ Himself and should find comfort in that truth. We need to accept this truth, own it, and hold fast to Christ.

But that's about as far as I am willing to carry this analogy. My old shirts were, after all, nothing more than old shirts that helped my daughters feel protected and comforted. In contrast, the protection afforded when we are clothed with Christ, according to Romans 13:12, is strong, like an 'armor of light.' As one translation renders Romans 13:12, 'Let Christ Jesus himself be the armor that you wear' (NEB). Unlike the shirts my daughters wore, Jesus is actually and really with us—and will ultimately keep us from being overcome by evil. Furthermore, Christ radiates light; He is compared to an 'armor of light,' which means we never need to be afraid of the dark. Paul extends the analogy yet further by explaining that if we have clothed ourselves with Christ (our armor of light) we should set aside the 'deeds of darkness' and 'make no provision for the flesh, to gratify its desires' (Rom. 13:12-14). You see, when you hold Christ close, the desire to participate in deeds of darkness diminishes.

Let me close this reflection with two questions: 1) Are you leaning into the security and comfort that comes from knowing the truth that you are clothed in Christ? 2) Are you holding Christ close? You have put on Christ and must stay close to Him as one who is clothed *in Christ*.

CHAPTER 23

BLESSED IN CHRIST

> 'Blessed be the God and Father of our Lord Jesus Christ, who has blessed us in Christ with every spiritual blessing in the heavenly places' (Eph. 1:3).

She always used the word 'blessed.' I'm not even sure she knew what it meant. But my maternal grandmother definitely liked that word. At least when I was nine years old I had good reason to believe she did. I heard it hundreds of times during the year she lived with our family. But I never quite figured out what she was talking about, and I secretly wondered whether she herself knew.

'Blessed' is a word Christians use a lot—but sometimes without really knowing what it means. It's not commonly used outside Christian circles, though occasionally you will hear someone make a comment like, 'I feel blessed.' But it's actually a powerhouse word. The Apostle Paul even made the decision to launch his extraordinary letter to the Ephesians using this word not only once, but twice in his opening volley of praise. Nevertheless, Paul uses it in two distinct ways.

'Blessed be the God and Father of our Lord Jesus Christ' (Eph. 1:3a). Paul's first use of the word 'blessed' in Ephesians 1 simply means 'praise.' He offers thanks to God. Then Paul continues his sentence: 'who has blessed us in Christ with every spiritual blessing in the heavenly places' (Eph. 1:3b). Here we encounter his second, and more complicated, meaning of the word 'blessed.' This use occurs at the precise moment when Paul launches his spiritual reflections into the stratosphere. What on earth does it mean to be blessed in Christ with every spiritual blessing in the heavenly places?

Paul uses this expression 'blessed us with every spiritual blessing' to explain that God has lavishly given us incredibly good things; that is, He has graced us with all sorts of spiritual benefits and advantages. But

Paul isn't writing about earthly goods like abundant food, stable work, a loving family, or a place to live; he is getting ramped up about spiritual realities. In other words, he focuses on all the good gifts God has granted us *spiritually,* which he describes as belonging to the heavenly realm rather than the earthly realm. These spiritual blessings are what permeate his first paragraph in Ephesians, and they read like a Table of Contents in a theology textbook: election, adoption, redemption, forgiveness, grace, inheritance, and sealing. These are the blessings with which we have been blessed!

But the most important thing Paul calls out in this sentence of praise is that these spiritual blessings are *in Christ.* It might be easy to gloss over this phrase, except for the fact that in this paragraph (1:3-14) Paul repeats the expression *in Christ,* or an expression like it (*in him, in the beloved*) eleven times. Eleven times! How much greater emphasis could he place on the truth that God hasn't just blessed us; He has blessed us with every spiritual blessing *in Christ.*

My grandmother wasn't perfect. She was, in truth, far from it. But God had rescued her out of a life of sin, scandal, and stacks of suffering, and she lived with an acute awareness that God's acceptance of her was an astounding *blessing.* Maybe she didn't understand all that it meant; I'm pretty sure she didn't. But she was mindful enough to keep praising God for the spiritual benefits—the blessings—she had received because of her connection to Jesus.

You too, dear friend, have been *blessed* with extraordinary and lavish spiritual blessings because you are *in Christ.*

CHAPTER 24

CHOSEN IN CHRIST

> 'he chose us in him before the foundation of the world, that we should be holy and blameless before him. In love he predestined us for adoption as sons through Jesus Christ, according to the purpose of his will' (Eph. 1:4-5).

As I start this chapter I am sitting in a large room at the Los Angeles County Courthouse with a couple hundred other potential jurors. Soon I will learn whether I have been selected to sit on a jury.

Is being chosen in Christ like that? Are we included because our name just happened to be the next randomly-selected name on the list? What about the selection process, is it impersonal? And what does God intend to do with us? Like pressing jurors into service, does God choose us merely with the aim of accomplishing His own goals, or does He also intend good for us?

In Ephesians 1:4-5, Paul offers enough hints to let us know how he would answer each of these questions. Briefly:

1) No, jury selection is not an adequate metaphor for election. Adoption is better.

2) No, we were not randomly selected. God specifically chose us.

3) No, election is not impersonal. God chose us 'in love.'

4) No, God doesn't use us merely to accomplish His inscrutable purposes; His loving intentions also include our transformation.

Over the course of nine years, Trudi and I set aside four separate periods to prayerfully consider whether we should adopt more children into our family. For various reasons, we didn't experience the Lord's confirmation to pursue adoption until the fourth extended period of prayer. Once we finally got our hearts lined up with the Lord and with each other, we pursued adoption with a passion.

We made a settled decision to adopt two precious daughters before we even met them. Take a moment and let that sink in. We didn't enter into this life-altering decision based upon background, or personality, or appearance, or even whether they decided to respond in love to us. We placed our love upon two little girls, ages 8 and 10, who needed a loving family because…well…not *because* at all. We simply set our love on them…before we met them…before they knew we existed!

In a similar (though not exactly parallel) way, Ephesians 1:4-5 says that God chose to direct His love toward us by adopting us. He made the decision to enter into this relationship for reasons we will never begin to understand, and unlike us, He possessed a comprehension of the implications of His choice that we can't begin to fathom. He chose us, not on the basis of anything at all about *us;* the basis of His selection was *Christ.* His decision to gather us into His family was far from impersonal; it required the loving sacrifice of His only Son! Not only did He accomplish His cosmic purposes, one of His goals in choosing each of us is that we would be 'holy and blameless before him.'

No wonder Paul keeps bursting out with praise in this section of Scripture! I'm having trouble holding in my praise in the middle of the jurors' room in the L.A. county courthouse.

OK. Jury selection is finished. I'm writing this final paragraph after the process is all over. You're probably wondering whether I got selected to sit on a jury. No, I was not chosen. It was a long day waiting around just to find out, but I am glad for the encouragement I received in the middle of a long day of waiting for jury selection as I reflected once again on God's lavish love in choosing to adopt me, not because of anything I did, but simply because He demonstrated extravagant generosity when He chose me *in Christ.*

CHAPTER 25

FORGIVEN IN CHRIST

> 'In him we have...the forgiveness of our trespasses' (Eph. 1:7).
>
> 'in whom we have redemption, the forgiveness of sins' (Col. 1:14).
>
> 'having forgiven us all our trespasses, by canceling the record of debt that stood against us with its legal demands. This he set aside, nailing it to the cross' (Col. 2:13b-14).

IN DEBT. For some people, those two words foment deep anxiety. They are a reminder of days when they couldn't pay off a credit card. Or a hospital bill. Or a crushing student loan. Sometimes those two words are a reminder that someone is currently in debt. As though anyone in debt needs someone to remind them!

I have heard of college seniors sitting through their own graduation ceremonies trembling in their seats as they reckon with the fact that they now have to quickly find a job to start paying off college loans. On a day when they should be celebrating the fact that they have just earned a college degree, they are quivering at the mountain of debt looming before them.

What if….? What if those massive loans could simply be forgiven? Completely done away with? Eradicated? Suppose there were a way to wipe away all of your own loans. Would you take the promissory note and light it on fire? Yes! Publicly and decisively.

But what if your indebtedness wasn't money? What if what you owed was righteousness? In other words, what if your debt was an obligation to be righteous in the sight of God, and the only way to pay it off was to live sinlessly for a day…no…for a lifetime? The problem with such a prospect is that you *know* you could never—will never—succeed in living sinlessly, even for a day. You are too familiar with yourself. You know your sins too well, including the secret thoughts of your heart.

You are trapped in debt, a debt from which you can never be released because the One to whom you owe your debt is Himself perfect, sinless, impeccable, and holy, and unfortunately, you and I are not.

This is why forgiveness in Christ is astounding, and why we must do all we can to allow its staggering reality to move us toward worship and responsive love. The extent of our indebtedness loomed larger than any student loan, hospital bill, or credit card balance. Then, for reasons that God alone in His infinite wisdom will ever understand, Jesus forgave all of it for those who put their trust in Him. He did it 'by canceling the record of debt that stood against us with its legal demands. This he set aside, nailing it to the cross' (Col. 2:14).

I love that final phrase! It is awful and beautiful at the same time. On the one hand, no thought is crueler than the picture of my beloved Savior hanging mid-air on a cross—paying my sin-debt. Nothing disturbs me more than the image of my Lord on a rough Roman beam with wrists pinned by a spike to a wooden crossbar. My alarm increases when I visualize a placard itemizing my sins attached to the same spike, smeared with His blood.

On the other hand, this image is more beautiful and compelling than any sight in the world. I know of nothing more magnificent than the self-sacrifice of my Lord. I allow myself to look more closely at the scene, and notice the words 'forgiven' stamped across my promissory note. When Jesus died on that dreadful cross, my record of sins died with Him. I bow my head—first in shame, then in deep gratitude.

This is why I love my Savior so. The sum total of my debt contained a figure infinitely larger than I could ever repay. But because of the self-sacrifice of my incessantly loving Savior, all my sins have been forgiven *in Christ*.

CHAPTER 26

SEATED WITH CHRIST

'according to the working of his great might that he worked in Christ when he raised him from the dead and seated him at his right hand in the heavenly places' (Eph. 1:19b-20).

'and raised us up with him and seated us with him in the heavenly places in Christ Jesus' (Eph. 2:6).

Honestly, do you sometimes read Paul's letters and find your eyes glazing over as you think: 'Paul, what are you talking about? I can understand that we were raised with Christ, and that we are sitting with Christ in the heavenly places! And I know that Jesus rose from the dead. Literally, in His body. Furthermore, since I have put my faith in Christ, I know that I will be raised in the future. Literally, in my body. But now, Paul, you're telling me that in some mysterious way that I have *already been raised*, and—even harder to understand—that I have *already sat down* with Christ in heaven? Seriously? What's going on here, Paul?'

Let me try to help you understand. Paul isn't saying that we have some duplicate body hanging out in heaven. Nor is he talking about a mystical out-of-body experience. When Paul claims that we have already been seated with Christ, he is making a truth-claim. It is a theological truth that is accompanied by profound implications for daily life.

The key is found in Ephesians 1. Immediately after Paul wrote that God 'raised him [Christ] from the dead and seated him at his right hand in the heavenly places,' Paul added the words: 'far above all rule and authority and power and dominion, and above every name that is named, not only in this age but also in the one to come' (Eph. 1:20-21). Since the words *rule, authority, power,* and *dominion* in Ephesians are shorthand for powerful evil spirits, Paul is asserting that because Jesus is seated in the heavenlies, He holds the position of power over every demonic spirit that might challenge His authority.

That was chapter 1 of Ephesians. In chapter 2, astonishingly, Paul connects this truth to us. When we believed, Paul tells us, we were seated with Christ in heavenly places.

Pause and follow Paul's logic:
- If Jesus is over all demonic challengers (seated above them),
- and if we are *in Christ* (sitting with Christ above those evil powers),
- then what is true of Christ is also true of us:
- we also have authority over Satan and his evil angels.

Thus, when we begin to 'walk' in the truths of our *inChristness,* using the analogy Paul will explicate in Ephesians 4–5, we can be certain that nothing will ever hinder us from learning how to walk the Christian walk. And when we 'stand' against the devil in the evil day, using the analogy that Paul is going to utilize in Ephesians 6, we can stand strong 'in the Lord and in the strength of his might' (6:10). When we truly learn and own the truth that we are sitting with Christ—that we have authority even over the strongest and most evil powers in the universe—we will rest in the confidence that nothing is strong enough to hinder us when we seek to 'walk' in daily life and 'stand' in the evil day.

But let me leave you with this reminder: We do not possess authority on our own. We only have authority because we are *in Christ.* That's what we saw in Ephesians 1–2. Apart from our *inChristness,* we would be defenseless against Satan and his powerful army of evil angels. But we truly have the right and power to live out our daily walk in Christ and to stand against the devil and his demons, because we are seated *in Christ.*

CHAPTER 27

GRACE IN CHRIST

> 'so that in the coming ages he might show the immeasurable riches of his grace in kindness toward us in Christ Jesus' (Eph. 2:7).
>
> 'not because of our works but because of his own purpose and grace, which he gave us in Christ Jesus before the ages began' (2 Tim. 1:9).
>
> 'You then, my child, be strengthened by the grace that is in Christ Jesus' (2 Tim. 2:1).

Let me introduce you to a prominent word in the New Testament. That word, in Greek, is *charis* (pronounced: kâr-is)—most commonly translated as 'grace.' It appears 155 times in the New Testament. The author who uses it most frequently, unsurprisingly, is the Apostle Paul. He was a man overwhelmed by the undeserved favor God had extended to him. He was on the road to Damascus to arrest followers of 'the Way' when Jesus literally knocked him off his feet with grace (Acts 9:4). Despite the fact that Paul had been persecuting Christians, God graciously forgave all he had done through Christ. Paul never stopped talking about and being thankful for the amazing grace he had received.

But let me tell you one thing you might not know about grace, or at least about the Greek word often translated as 'grace' in our Bibles. The word *charis* is used in the New Testament both for what God does for us (He shows us *undeserved favor*) as well as for what our response to Him should be (we respond in *thankfulness*). The same word (*charis*) gets used both for God's grace toward us and for our gratitude to God.

And therein lies a nugget of insight about how we should respond to God's grace. The appropriate response to grace (*charis*) is giving thanks (*charis*). Do you want to understand—truly understand—God's grace better than you do now? Respond to God's grace with continual, repeated, frequent gratitude—over and over again.

Like Paul did. Sometimes he was so taken with the grace of God that he burst out in exclamations of gratitude, even in contexts where you wouldn't expect it. Like:

'Thanks (*charis*) be to God through Jesus Christ our Lord!' (Rom. 7:25);

'Thanks (*charis*) be to God for his inexpressible gift!' (2 Cor. 9:15);

'But thanks (*charis*) be to God, who gives us the victory through our Lord Jesus Christ!' (1 Cor. 15:57).

Now, Paul certainly could have used other words beside *charis* for giving thanks—and he often did. But Paul insistently grounded his gratitude in the undeserved grace given to him and to all believers. Here's an example: 'I give thanks [a different Greek word] to my God always for you because of the grace (*charis*) of God that was given you in Christ Jesus' (1 Cor. 1:4). Do you see the strong connection between grace and thanks in this verse?

Let me repeat something I just wrote: If you want to understand the grace of God better, give thanks a lot.

But isn't that too simple? I'm already thankful that God showed me grace through Jesus! What else would I be?

Selfish. Forgetful. Lazy. Hesitant to speak words of thanks. Like I often am.

But there is more to say about grace than this. The Apostle Paul taught that we are 'strengthened by the grace that is in Christ Jesus' (2 Tim. 2:1). Donald Guthrie comments, '*Grace* here has the usual Pauline meaning of unmerited favour, but includes within it the divine enabling.'[12] Not only do we increasingly *comprehend* grace by responding with the appropriate response—thankfulness; we are somehow strengthened by the grace we have received *in Christ*.

God has shown us undeserved favor (*charis*) in Jesus. The appropriate response is gratitude. He also strengthens us through that grace. All this is because we are *in Christ*.

CHAPTER 28

MYSTERY OF CHRIST

'When you read this, you can perceive my insight into the mystery of Christ, which was not made known to the sons of men in other generations as it has now been revealed to his holy apostles and prophets by the Spirit. This mystery is that the Gentiles are fellow heirs, members of the same body, and partakers of the promise in Christ Jesus through the gospel' (Eph. 3:4-6).

'that their hearts may be encouraged, being knit together in love, to reach all the riches of full assurance of understanding and the knowledge of God's mystery, which is Christ, in whom are hidden all the treasures of wisdom and knowledge' (Col. 2:2-3).

A number of years ago I downloaded to my e-reader a free collection of G. K. Chesterton's Father Brown mysteries. In Chesterton's stories, Father Brown solves crimes while still serving his parish as a priest. Sometimes Father Brown requests his friends to trust him when he is trying to solve a particularly intransigent crime, without giving any explanation of how his plan will resolve the mystery. When he asks for their help, they have no idea how he will expose the perpetrator or bring resolution to the investigation.

The Apostle Paul also wrote about a mystery, the solution of which, he said, had been unknown until his generation. That mystery had to do with how Gentiles got included alongside Jews into God's plan of salvation.

But it's important to notice what Paul did *not* say about the mystery. He did not deny that the prophets had already openly declared that God would provide a plan of salvation for Gentiles. Akin to how Father Brown sometimes announces a solution without explaining how it will work out, the prophets had already prophesied that God would bring salvation to the Gentiles. Paul certainly knew about the Old Testament promises (Rom. 15:8-12), so it wasn't a mystery in that respect. The mysterious portion was found in the *means* and *manner* by which God would bring Gentiles into His plan. Paul disclosed that Gentiles would be offered salvation—full acceptance with God on the same level as Jews who believed in Jesus—*without having first to convert to Judaism and be circumcised.*[13]

The mystery wasn't in the *what.* The mystery was in the *how.* The revelation was that Gentiles got included without converting to Judaism through what Messiah Jesus did on the cross. This was entirely unexpected to many first-century Jews, including some Jews who believed in Jesus.

So if the mystery has already been revealed, it isn't a mystery that we need to try to solve anymore. That is, it isn't a mystery anymore.

There were some teachers in the second and third centuries A.D. who claimed to be Christians (but were not) and who tried to convince people that salvation came through *knowing* secret things that other people didn't know—solving spiritual mysteries. Today we call these people Gnostics. But Paul would strongly disagree with anything that smacked of Gnosticism. The mystery is not something we have to try to figure out. Paul says that the mystery has already been revealed. The mystery was *how* God could bring Gentiles into the same plan of salvation that He had set out for the Jews, and we now know the solution to that mystery.

It is a mystery no longer. The solution to how Jews and Gentiles can be saved and united together *is* Christ. I am connected to you, and you to me—Jew or Gentile—because everyone who has believed is *in Christ.*

CHAPTER 29

FOUND IN CHRIST

> 'that I may gain Christ and be found in him, not having a righteousness of my own that comes from the law, but that which comes through faith in Christ' (Phil. 3:8b-9).

In the middle of one of my all-time favorite biblical passages, Philippians 3:7-14, Paul employs an unusual expression. He says that he wants to be *found in Christ*, which initially doesn't make much sense. The phrase starts to make a tiny bit of sense when you observe that in the previous sentences, Paul has remarked three times how he considers everything to be *loss*—a word that might work with *finding* something—so that he might *gain* Christ. But doesn't it still seem strange for Paul to say that he wants to be 'found' in Christ? I mean, if someone wants to communicate the same longing and hope of *gaining Christ* using the language of *finding*, shouldn't he say that he aims to *find Christ* instead of be *found in Christ?*

Paul probably chooses to write *found in Christ* instead of *find Christ* to make sure we don't fail to grasp a truth that is easily misunderstood. Paul doesn't want anyone to think that he is taking any credit for getting into his special relationship with God. Christ gets all the credit for that. Saying *found in him* rather than *finding him* circumvents such a misunderstanding, and points out the truth that a right standing with God is accomplished entirely through Christ.

But even then, it is unusual for someone to say that he wants to be found *in* someone else. What does it mean to be found in Christ? Understanding this is profound. Paul is saying that at the end of the age, on the final day of reckoning, it will become known to all that he was connected to Christ.

I recently heard about a 14-year-old boy who hid with his two small brothers in a walk-in closet while their house was being robbed. The robbers ransacked two rooms and took off with the family's money-box. But when the police arrived they *found* the boys still in the closet—the younger boys still shielded by the teen, who, incidentally, had a weapon aimed at the closet door!

The *found in Christ* language is like the location of those little boys. Paul wants everyone to know that he has been with Christ the whole time. Paul knows that he has no more ability to save himself than little boys have in protecting themselves from ransacking thieves. No works of righteousness offer him any hope; his basis of expectancy for the future is faith in Christ (Phil. 3:9). Paul longs for the day when all that Christ has done will be displayed for everyone to see—when he will be found in Christ. I can almost hear those little boys exclaiming after their harrowing experience, 'Our big brother saved us! The police found us hiding with him. He protected us!' Similarly, Paul looks forward with eager anticipation to the day when the fact of his *inChristness* will become known to all.

How about you? Do you long to be *found* in Christ? Do you look forward to the proclamation that you have been with Christ the whole time? One take-away from this discussion is that most of us need to increase our longing for what the final day will reveal about our connectedness to Christ. Even if everything around us falls apart, being in Christ guarantees that we will be *found* safe and secure with Him at the end of it all. Have you begun to look forward to the day when all this gets exposed—when everyone in heaven and earth will know that you were delivered because you were found *in Christ*?

CHAPTER 30

UPWARD CALL OF GOD IN CHRIST

> 'Not that I have already obtained this or am already perfect, but I press on to make it my own, because Christ Jesus has made me his own. Brothers, I do not consider that I have made it my own. But one thing I do: forgetting what lies behind and straining forward to what lies ahead, I press on toward the goal for the prize of the upward call of God in Christ Jesus' (Phil. 3:12-14).

During the past two weeks (at the time of this writing), my family has been following the world's greatest sporting event—the Olympic Games. There is one thing consistent about the various contests we've watched. At the end of each competition, the winning athletes are called up to a pedestal to receive a prize. Thus it has always been, all the way back to the first Olympic Games in ancient Greece. Those who win are *called up* to receive their awards.

When Paul wrote that he pressed on toward the goal for the prize of the *upward call* of God in Christ Jesus, it is not entirely clear what Paul meant by the 'upward call' (or 'heavenly call' in some translations). But a plausible suggestion is that Paul was looking forward to the final day when he would be summoned by God to a victor's pedestal.[14] Notice the imagery in these verses (Phil. 3:12-14): *pressing on, straining forward, what lies ahead, the goal, the prize*—all of which suggest a running race, a race that culminates in an upward call to a podium to receive a prize.

Somewhat surprisingly, Paul refers to the race that leads to this awards ceremony as the 'one thing I do' (3:13). Every time I read those words, I find myself mentally pushing back, 'Seriously, Paul, only one thing? You traveled, made tents, studied, wrote letters...' But Paul would undoubtedly retort: 'No, the other things were peripheral. The in-Christ life that God called me to was my central passion. I strained forward and pressed on to know Christ.'

But what does *inChristness* have to do with this life of fervent pursuit? For Paul, it had *everything* to do with it! Paul made plain that he didn't think of himself as accomplishing anything. Far more important than how he ran (and he *did* run!) was that 'Christ Jesus has made me his own' (3:12). Consequently, at the end of the race, he knew that he could take no credit whatsoever for successfully finishing the race. When God summons someone to the pedestal, the upward call is *in Christ Jesus* (3:14).

Allow me a moment of speculation. Is it possible that Paul pictured his walk to the victor's pedestal not as a solitary ascent, but with Christ walking beside him? Is this why he described the upward call as being *in Christ Jesus*? Everywhere else in his letters he emphasized that he was *in Christ* during his entire earthly run. Throughout all those long years, through deserts and over seemingly insurmountable mountains, when the race seemed interminable and days of running were desperately lonely, he remembered that there was one running alongside him.

Might it be that when you look back at the highlight reel of your life, you too will discover that Christ was running with you the entire time? Will you see that when you tripped and fell, Christ was the One who lifted you, even when you didn't know it? When you ran free and fast, will you discover that He was the One pulling you forward, even when you didn't feel it?

Then, when you finally get summoned to the victor's podium, Christ will be right beside you—since He was always with you anyway. You will be called to the platform, receiving your *upward call,* because—and only because—you were, are, and always will be *in Christ.*

CHAPTER 31

REDEMPTION IN CHRIST

'He has delivered us from the domain of darkness and transferred us to the kingdom of his beloved Son, in whom we have redemption' (Col. 1:13-14).

'who gave himself for us to redeem us from all lawlessness and to purify for himself a people for his own possession who are zealous for good works' (Titus 2:14).

'through the redemption that is in Christ Jesus' (Rom. 3:24).

Whenever you encounter the word 'redemption,' biblical bells ought to start ringing in your head. (What is a biblical bell, you ask? A biblical bell is an alert that you need to connect something you've just read to somewhere else in the Bible. People who read the Bible a lot hear bells ringing in their heads all the time.) Here's what should start ringing in your head whenever you read the word 'redemption':

Biblical Bell #1: If someone you cared about was sold into slavery and you wanted to buy him or her out of slavery, you would have to pay the price of redemption (Lev. 25:47-52). This is the most basic meaning of redemption: being bought out of slavery.

Biblical Bell #2: God brought the children of Israel out of slavery in Egypt. The Bible describes this as redeeming them from their slavery (Exod. 6:6). Release from slavery in Egypt was Israel's redemption.

Biblical Bell #3: Boaz redeemed Ruth when he exercised his right as kinsman-redeemer and paid the redemption price to acquire all that belonged to Naomi's deceased husband (Ruth 2:20; 3:9-13; 4:3-11). In so doing, he released Naomi and Ruth out of their desperate plight as widows living in Israel, somewhat akin to slavery during the desperate period of the judges. Of course, Boaz ended up with a wife in the process!

So anytime you see the word 'redemption' in the New Testament, biblical bells ought to go off that remind you that Paul is not just using high-falutin theological language, as many people think when they read the word 'redemption,' but that he is alluding to the larger theme in the Bible of purchase-out-of-slavery.

So what are we redeemed—or purchased—out of, according to Paul? Paul mentions two things: 1) we are redeemed from lawlessness (Titus 2:14), and 2) we are redeemed out of the kingdom of darkness (Col. 1:13-14). This means that neither sin nor Satan has a hold on us anymore. That's an encouraging thought, isn't it?

But redemption isn't merely *out of* something. We have been redeemed from lawlessness—yes, indeed!, but we have also been purified and made into a people that God possesses (Titus 2:14). We have been redeemed out of the kingdom of darkness, but we have now been transferred into the kingdom of the Son (Col. 1:13-14)!

So, brother or sister, you need to remember this when you go to work tomorrow and feel alone, as though you're the only one in this 'kingdom.' You need to keep your redemption in mind when you sit in a classroom in which a teacher celebrates immorality. If you find yourself with some unexpected free time some evening, you need to tie into the truth that you have been redeemed from lawlessness and no longer belong in the kingdom of darkness; thus, pursuing sin outside the in-Christ life is not your lot. When you feel unexpected anxiety— or even true fear—in the middle of the night, you need to remember that you have been released from the power of sin and Satan by the Lord Jesus Himself, who purchased you with His blood.

This means that our destiny is interconnected with His life rather than to anything that might have bound us in the past. It is true that in the past we were inextricably united to sin and Satan. But now we are attached to Christ.

Maybe…just maybe…we can start living like it. We have been redeemed *in Christ*.

CHAPTER 32

ROOTED IN CHRIST

'rooted and built up in him and established in the faith' (Col. 2:7).

'And it is God who establishes us with you in Christ' (2 Cor. 1:21).

'stand firm thus in the Lord, my beloved' (Phil. 4:1).

'May the Lord direct your hearts...to the steadfastness of Christ' (2 Thess. 3:5).

Have you ever tried to uproot a tree? I don't mean a little one…

I remember as a teenager helping my dad remove an old and less-than-healthy cherry tree that sat in the middle of the front lawn of our family home in San Jose, California. All of us were tired of stepping on cherries every time we walked up the front walkway and decided it was time for the tree to go. So we started by removing all the branches, and left only a large branchless trunk sticking out of the ground like a totem pole. Next, we dug a deep ditch around the bottom of the tree, severing as many roots as we could cut. Finally, we tied one end of a heavy-duty rope to the top of the twenty-foot trunk and the other to the frame of our family station wagon…

I will never forget watching the back wheels of that station wagon *lift off the ground* as my dad tried to pull that cherry tree out of the ground. Now, mind you, this wasn't just any old station wagon. No siree! Dad didn't want to try to merge onto the highway in a sluggish car, so he installed a Chevy 454 big block engine—yes, in the family car! And even though we had enough horsepower in that car to beat back every drag racer in our city, that tree refused to budge until we spent a lot more time digging it out.

I want my life as a Christian to be like that cherry tree, don't you? I want to be 'rooted and built up in him and established in the faith' as

Paul writes about in Colossians 2:7. I want to be like the tree of Psalm 1 that is 'planted by streams of water,' and not like the wicked who are 'chaff that the wind drives away' (1:3-4). I want to be established in Christ (2 Cor. 1:21), standing firm in the Lord (Phil. 4:1) and having a heart directed to the steadfastness of Christ (2 Thess. 3:5). In short, I want to be a man who lives as though I am rooted in Christ, since in fact I am rooted in Him! And I pray that you do too.

Then when someone starts promulgating false doctrine, like they did in Colosse, claiming that Jesus isn't enough and that you need something more than Jesus if you really want to succeed spiritually (Col. 2:8, 16-23), you will be so rooted in Christ that you won't pay attention to their claims. And when hardship comes your way because of your Christian testimony, or when suffering comes knocking at your door simply because you are a member of the human race, you will remain steadfast in Christ. And when you are falsely accused and shunned and dishonored and overlooked and snubbed, even though any observer would attest that you are seeking to live a God-honoring and righteous life, you will press your roots even deeper into Christ, and draw all the sustenance you need from the soil where your roots make their home, that is, from Christ.

For, you see, you are connected to Christ the way our stubborn cherry tree was connected to the soil. But unlike that cherry tree which finally came out after hours of struggling to uproot it, there is nothing whatsoever that can dislodge you, no power that can move you, and no force that can remove you since you are rooted *in Christ.*

CHAPTER 33

CIRCUMCISED BY CHRIST

> 'In him also you were circumcised with a circumcision made without hands, by putting off the body of the flesh, by the circumcision of Christ' (Col. 2:11).

Some content may be inappropriate for young children. So begin some news pieces. In a rather uninhibited statement, the Apostle Paul compares our *inChristness* to circumcision.

For some reason lost on most Bible readers, God chose to identify a people, the children of Israel, as His own by commanding them to snip off a piece of skin from the most private and sensitive body part of every male. This sign of the covenant was a daily reminder of their distinctiveness from the nations surrounding them who did not worship the one true God.

But God never intended circumcision to be merely physical. God wanted His people to circumcise their *hearts* as well (Deut. 10:16; Jer. 4:4), which opened the door for including everyone who believed, Jew or Gentile, in the people of God, since 'circumcision is a matter of the heart' (Rom. 2:29).

So when Paul declares in Colossians 2:11, 'In him [Christ] you were circumcised with a circumcision made without hands, by putting off the body of the flesh, by the circumcision of Christ,' he is carrying the analogy of spiritual circumcision one further step. Not only is circumcision a matter of the heart (which is the point of calling it a circumcision 'made without hands'), spiritual circumcision disconnects you from your attachment to sin.

Now, please understand, Paul is not denying that you *feel* attached to sin. But that's a psychological notion. Paul's point is that you *actually aren't* trapped in sin anymore. This is because the Israelites of old probably assumed that the piece of skin that got sliced off was inextricably linked to sin for those who still had it, and inevitably led to sinning. Let me explain.

The nations around Israel were immoral, both literally and metaphorically, and the men of those nations still had foreskins. The sign of the covenant, circumcision, was intended as a constant reminder to everyone in Israel not to be 'immoral,' which in the Old Testament included sexual immorality, but was also regularly linked to worshiping idols (Deut. 7:3-4; Exod. 34:16; Josh. 23:6-13). So every time a man looked down at his circumcision, he was reminded that he didn't have to be immoral because he was cut off from immorality and connected by covenant to God. It's as though an uncircumcised person who still had his foreskin would have been viewed as *inevitably* immoral—certain to be pulled into idolatry. Cutting off the foreskin was a sign that idolatry was no longer inevitable (though, of course, an Israelite could still choose to commit sin after the sign-of-inevitability was removed). Cutting off the foreskin probably reminded an Israelite that he did not have to follow the ways of the surrounding nations because he had been joined by a covenantal act to the one true God.

Following this thematic strand, Paul declares that those who have been joined to Christ in spiritual circumcision have had the power of sin cut away. This is probably the same spiritual idea Paul wrote about in Romans 6:6 (using a different analogy) when he declared that someone who has died to sin doesn't have to keep living in it.

In other words, if our 'foreskin,' which signifies our inevitable attachment to sinning, is removed, we no longer are obliged to sin.

I once had a younger college student tell me, 'I just can't stop myself from sinning in this particular way.' But the Bible declares otherwise. Our attachment to sin has been removed, which means that succumbing to temptation is no longer inevitable. We have been spiritually circumcised, and therefore do not have to give in to sin any longer. Why? Because we have been joined to Christ. Our spiritual circumcision is *in Christ*.

CHAPTER 34

HIDDEN WITH CHRIST IN GOD

'your life is hidden with Christ in God' (Col 3:3).

A hymn I learned as a child was running through my mind. I was perched on the side of a mountain overlooking the town of Idyllwild, California—one of my favorite places to pray. I had set aside this time for prayer because I sensed a spiritual storm on the horizon. Here is the chorus of that hymn:

He hideth my soul in the cleft of the rock
That shadows a dry, thirsty land
He hideth my life in the depths of His love
And covers me there with His hand.[15]

As I prayed with the help of the hymn I turned around and looked up the steep incline behind me, and—unbelievably—my eyes actually fixed upon a cleft (that is, a small cave-like shelter) under a rock protruding from the side of the mountain. I was sure that God put it there for me!

So even though I'm not an experienced climber, I spent the next twenty minutes scraping and scratching my way up the steep incline until I finally settled into an actual cleft of a rock. I sat in that natural alcove for about two hours, praying as I watched literal storm clouds gather on the horizon and thinking about many saints in the past who were hidden and protected by God in rocky clefts.

I thought about Moses, whose story formed the basis for the hymn, who got so caught up in responding to God's greatness that he blurted out a request to see the glory of God. The Lord, of course, couldn't allow Moses to see His face since it would have killed Moses, but lovingly placed him in—yes!—the cleft of a rock and shielded him with His hand while He passed by, and then lifted His hand so Moses could get a momentary glimpse of the glory of God (Exod. 33:18-23).

I also thought...as I prayed...about the story (actually, a tiny story within the broader Elijah narrative) of Obadiah (1 Kings 18:3-4—not the prophet of the same name), a God-fearing man who hid and fed a hundred prophets of God in two caves while Jezebel was trying to eradicate all of God's prophets from the land of Israel. I imagined myself as one of those prophets, protected in the cave while waiting out the wrath of Jezebel.

I thought about Elijah who received a renewed ministry-call from the Lord after fleeing from Jezebel and hiding in yet a different cave. God met him on the mountain outside that cave by sending a soft blowing, a hushed whisper of the awesome God of tornados, earthquakes, and fire, but who chose that day to draw in Elijah with gentleness (1 Kings 19).

I recalled the snippet in Hebrews 11:38 about the faith-filled followers who hid out 'in dens and caves of the earth.' I thought about the underground cities I had visited in Turkey where ancient Christians found refuge from their persecutors.

And I meditated as I prayed on the truth that because I have been raised with Christ, my life is permanently 'hidden with Christ in God' (Col. 3:3). *In Christ,* I am concealed from the evil spirits seeking to harm me, and protected from the malevolent machinations of earthly evildoers. No evil can reach me because I am hidden in Christ. God strengthened my heart with these thoughts.

I emerged from that cleft of the rock ready to descend to the valley below, especially since I could see a (literal) storm about to break. The best part of it all is that I knew that even if I got caught in the storm (literal or figurative) I would *still* be hidden with Christ in God. It is a firm and secure reality because I am *in Christ.*

2
DAILY LIFE
IN CHRIST

CHAPTER 35

CONFORMED TO THE IMAGE OF CHRIST

'For those whom he fore-knew he also predestined to be conformed to the image of his Son, in order that he might be the firstborn among many brothers' (Rom. 8:29).

'and have put on the new self, which is being renewed in knowledge after the image of its creator' (Col. 3:10).

This chapter is not about predestination, even if that's the first thing my students want to talk about when they encounter Romans 8:29. Suffice it to say that predestination is important to me; I gladly dive deep—at least as deep as I can—into this doctrine with my students. But an analysis of predestination isn't the purpose of this book. This book's goal is to help us understand how *inChristness* connects with life, and Romans 8:29 is one signpost pointing us in the right direction.

Romans 8:29 explains that God not only knew ahead of time, but also purposed that those He justified would be 'conformed to the image of his Son.' God, expressing lavish, undeserved love, decided not only to call, justify, and glorify us (Rom 8:30), He planned to shape us into the likeness of Christ—to make us like Christ.

Travel with me in your thoughts to eternity past. God has just announced His decision to create a world filled with people. He didn't have to. As Father, Son, and Holy Spirit He was perfectly happy without humans around. But He also knew that creating people would be *good*, which is what He joyfully exclaimed after each day of creation. But unlike all the other things He had made during the first five days of creation, He molded humans into something more like Himself than anything else He had created. 'Then God said, "Let us make man in our image, after our likeness. And let them have dominion…" So God created man in his own image, in the image of God he created him; male and female he created them' (Gen. 1:26-27).

But as you know, humans fell, and great was their fall. Sin entered the world, and the image of God in humans was marred. Twisted. Distorted. It wasn't obliterated. That's why a human has no right to take someone else's life; humans were created in the image of God (Gen. 9:6). But Adam and Eve—and we too as their offspring—were spiritually disfigured when we allowed sin in.

God continued to tenaciously prepare the way for His children to share His image, despite the fall. And when God intends something, you can be sure that it will happen. He sent Jesus, God-in-the-flesh, the perfect image of God, to re-call, re-form, re-shape, re-create us… into the image of Christ. Even as some children increasingly resemble their parents as they get older, so God's intended outcome was that we would begin to look more and more like Christ.

If you ever find yourself wondering why God allows suffering to invade your life, remind yourself that God's highest purpose for you is not your comfort, but to conform you to Christ's image. If you ever wonder why your prayers don't get answered quickly —and find yourself groaning under that realization (Rom. 8:23-26)—recollect that God is remaking you into His image as He did with the first humans on the sixth day of creation. If you find that relationships are hard, that days are long, and that you haven't reached the goals you set for yourself when you were young, remember that God's primary goal for you is probably different from your youthful goals. His goal for you is Christlikeness. He is unwavering in His commitment to shape you into the image of Christ. He won't stop until He has accomplished His purposes in you. You can deeply rest in that knowledge. He will conform you to the image of Christ because He has called you *in Christ*.

CHAPTER 36

TELLING THE TRUTH IN CHRIST

'I am speaking the truth in Christ—I am not lying; my conscience bears me witness in the Holy Spirit' (Rom. 9:1).

'As the truth of Christ is in me' (2 Cor. 11:10).

'Rather, speaking the truth in love, we are to grow up in every way into him who is the head, into Christ' (Eph. 4:15).

An ironic incident occurred while I was living in the Middle East. We were trying to establish a church in a city where no church existed, and only a few nationals had yet come to faith. But one young man with whom I was meeting (Ozzie, not his real name) seemed to be on the verge of believing, while another young man was also showing serious interest in the gospel (Junee, again not his real name). But at the time, neither of the two had yet met the other. One day I was talking with Ozzie in a small office when Junee unexpectedly showed up and joined the conversation. Surprisingly, Ozzie began trying to persuade Junee to accept the Christian message—and Junee seemed to be responding positively! Within a couple of months, both men had made professions of faith and started meeting with the handful of new believers in the city.

But here's where the story takes an ironic and somewhat ugly twist. Both Ozzie and Junee were lying about everything. They were *both* infiltrators. Ozzie was informing for the police, Junee for a nationalist-fundamentalist group. Everything that had transpired between the two of them in that downtown office—everything!—was fake. What makes it so ironic is that at the time, I don't think that either knew the other was pretending! (I don't know whether to laugh or cry at this point...)

Now, God eventually exposed their duplicity and protected the infant Christian fellowship. But those two men were the first of a dozen or so people I have known for whom lying is both deliberate and chronic.

Lying, if you haven't yet realized it, is one of the worst relational sins. A meaningful friendship between two people cannot develop when deceit is present. Truth-telling, on the other hand, supports lasting relationships. But it goes deeper for a Christian. Truth-telling, according to the Apostle Paul, is *in Christ* (Rom. 9:1; 2 Cor. 11:10). We don't simply try to say what is true because we fear hurting the other person or negatively affecting our relationship. We speak truth in the presence of Christ, knowing that we are united with Christ by faith. And when we are habitually speaking the truth in love (literally, 'truthing in love'), the Bible says that we grow up even more *into* Christ (Eph. 4:15).

But how is it that *inChristness* has any bearing on truth-telling? Short answer: Christ *is* the *Truth* (capital T). He is the One who declares, 'I am the way, the truth, and the life' (John 14:6). Today we live in a relativistic age when people think that they can acquire a personal 'truth' different from the truth of others. That proves, by the way, that they know nothing about truth. But Jesus proclaims that He is the standard by which all other affirmations, whether substantial or mundane, must be measured.

How are you doing with telling the truth? Do you ever hide behind dishonest words? Do you occasionally bend the truth to protect yourself, further your agenda, or make yourself look good? A few of us may have started down that slippery slope which starts with a few 'innocent' half truths, but can end in a state of chronic lying. Those of us in that category might need to reach out to a wise Christian who can help us learn about our in-Christ identity and how to grow into a Christ-dependent life of truth. Remember, at its core, Christian truth-telling is speaking the truth *in Christ*.

CHAPTER 37

BOASTING IN CHRIST

> 'So I boast in Christ Jesus about the things that pertain to God' (Rom. 15:17 NET).
>
> 'But far be it from me to boast except in the cross of our Lord Jesus Christ, by which the world has been crucified to me, and I to the world' (Gal. 6:14).
>
> 'so that, as it is written, "Let the one who boasts, boast in the Lord"' (1 Cor. 1:31; 2 Cor. 10:17).

Nobody likes to be around someone who brags.

I remember one conversation where the only words I uttered were 'Hi' and 'How are you?' before the young man in front of me launched into a lengthy account of why he was dressed so sharply that day, where he had purchased his clothes, what a good price he had paid for them despite their obvious quality, how good he was at saving money on clothes, and how much better dressed he was than others at the event. This monologue was distressing, to say the least.

Nobody—I mean *nobody*—likes to be around someone who brags.

Psychologists tell us that most forms of bragging are unwelcome by others, with a few exceptions. The Apostle Paul would agree. You shouldn't boast in your good works (Eph. 2:9), or that you are better than someone else (Gal. 5:26), or that you have been given more spiritual blessings than others (1 Cor. 4:7). You shouldn't brag that your church leader is better than others (1 Cor. 3:21-22), or that people are easily influenced by you (Gal. 6:13). Paul twice refers to a famous passage about boasting in Jeremiah where that faithful but sorrowful prophet declared that it is inappropriate to brag about one's own wisdom, strength, or riches (Jer. 9:23-24; 1 Cor. 1:31; 2 Cor. 10:17).

So why does Paul 'boast' so much himself? A student once told me that he didn't like Paul because Paul was a braggart. In one sense he was correct, Paul does mention 'boasting' occasionally, but not in the way my student thought. Primarily, Paul 'boasted' about Jesus and the cross (Gal. 6:14). Imagine that yours had been one of the first lives saved by the twentieth century's new medical breakthrough, penicillin. Wouldn't you want to tell others about this super-drug so they could be saved too? You might even become an activist in promoting penicillin! Confident proclamation of Christ and salvation through the cross was Paul's primary area of 'boasting.' No Christian can call that kind of 'boasting' inappropriate. Like Paul, we can and should assertively proclaim Christ and the cross.

Paul was also happy to 'boast' about Christians who were generous with their finances (2 Cor. 9:2) and faithful in ministry (2 Cor. 7:14). Elsewhere, he drew attention to his own weaknesses, and for some reason decided to call it 'boasting in weakness,' which is not boasting at all, in fact; just the opposite (2 Cor. 11:30; 12:5, 9). Additionally, toward the end of 2 Corinthians, Paul defended his God-appointed credentials as an apostle—not because he wanted to, but because he believed that the work of God was being undermined through the attack on him. He defended his apostolic calling in order to protect the integrity of the gospel (2 Cor. 10:8-17; 11:16-19).

But as I've just mentioned, the most important area of 'boasting' for Paul was Christ Himself and all that Christ did to secure redemption and release through the cross. Paul gloried in Christ, talked about Him all the time, and shared Jesus Christ with everyone He could. If Paul calls this 'boasting,' that is fine by me. I only hope that I too will confidently proclaim Christ, promoting not myself, but my Lord. But we mustn't forget that the subject of our boasting should be Christ, and the only grounds for our boasting should be that we are *in Christ*.

CHAPTER 38

WORK IN CHRIST

'Greet those workers in the Lord, Tryphaena and Tryphosa. Greet the beloved Persis, who has worked hard in the Lord' (Rom. 16:12).

'Therefore, my beloved brothers, be steadfast, immovable, always abounding in the work of the Lord, knowing that in the Lord your labor is not in vain' (1 Cor. 15:58).

'Working together with him' (2 Cor. 6:1).

'remembering before our God and Father your work of faith and labor of love and steadfastness of hope in our Lord Jesus Christ' (1 Thess. 1:3).

My first three years as a full-time professor were spent in the New York City area. Unfortunately, 'spent' may be the right word to describe how I sometimes felt during that period. I was teaching a full load of classes five days a week and serving on the staff of a local church as a part-time worship pastor. My wife and two young daughters depended on me to spend quality time with them and bring home a paycheck. It won't surprise you to learn that I often felt very tired. Please don't misunderstand. I was deeply grateful for the opportunities God had given me. I was repeatedly the recipient of God's sustaining grace. I even observed God blessing my labors. But I was still tired. Frequently. And when I get tired, I sometimes secretly start to imagine that all my labors are in vain.

Has *work* ever made you tired? 'There's a reason it's called "work"!' commented an older business owner I know when he heard a younger man complaining about how hard his job was. Yes, it is work after all.

But does this mean we should just grit our teeth and get back to work? Is there any difference in how a Christian and a non-Christian respond to the tiredness of work?

One key difference is that we as Christians can remember that we labor *in the Lord*. Whether our work is located in a secular or a sacred setting (such distinctions aren't biblical anyway), whether we get paid for our work or serve without pay, whether we work in the public eye or at home, all work is to be done *in the Lord*.

Imagine that one day you arrived at your place of work only to discover that Jesus Himself had been hired as your co-worker. I'll bet that your workplace would feel different from how it does now. Not only would you want to do your work in a way that made Jesus proud, I imagine that knowing He was working with you would give you more strength to do your work. The fact remains: because of our *inChristness,* we are 'working together with him' (2 Cor. 6:1). Whatever work we do—whether as a professor, plumber, painter, producer, pilot, poet, preacher, or parent—can be done *for* Christ, *with* Christ, and *in* Christ.

Tryphaena, Tryphosa, and Persis were three women serving among the Christians in Rome. Since all three of their names were common slave names, biblical scholars assume that these women were probably slaves or former slaves. If correct, then they knew better than most of us what it was to be tired from work! But Paul described Tryphaena and Tryphosa as 'workers in the Lord,' and wrote that Persis 'has worked hard in the Lord' (Rom. 16:12). Paul viewed their service as 'in the Lord.' How fortunate the church in Rome was to have three women who modeled working in partnership with Christ!

Are you laboring under your labor? Are you worn-out by your work? You will come to know the strength and encouragement of the Lord as you remember that you work *in Christ*. You can be 'always abounding in the work of the Lord, knowing that in the Lord your labor is not in vain' (1 Cor. 15:58). Your work, brother or sister, is not in vain, because you are *in Christ.*

CHAPTER 39

SANCTIFICATION IN CHRIST

'To the church of God that is in Corinth, to those sanctified in Christ Jesus, called to be saints' (1 Cor. 1:2).

'even as he chose us in him before the foundation of the world, that we should be holy and blameless before him' (Eph. 1:4).

'who gave himself for us to redeem us from all lawlessness and to purify for himself a people for his own possession who are zealous for good works' (Titus 2:14).

Sanctification. A six-syllable word. A term that only theologians need to know. Something that pertains to saints, but probably doesn't apply to me.

There is only one correct statement in that paragraph: sanctification is indeed a word that pertains to saints. But 'saints' means something different from what many people think it means. Moreover, sanctification is a term that is not only important for theologians. It is pertinent for all Christians. Finally, the word sanctification only has five syllables, not six!

Normally in Christian theology, the word sanctification is used to describe the Christian's growth into a holy life, including increasing avoidance of sinful thoughts and actions. If you took a theology class at a seminary, you would notice that the term most commonly focuses on the moral aspects of the Christian life: separation from sins of passion, selfishness, pride, and the growth of a life increasingly dedicated to God.

This is all entirely correct, of course, but the Apostle Paul uses the word sanctification and all the words related to it (like 'sanctified,' 'holy,' and 'saints') in two main ways, not just one. And therein lies a precious secret for living out the in-Christ life.

When Paul writes about sanctification (sometimes translated as 'holiness' in our Bibles), he sometimes writes about *positional sanctification*, and other times about *progressive sanctification*. He greets the church in Corinth with these words: 'To the church of God that is in Corinth, to those sanctified in Christ Jesus, called to be saints' (1 Cor. 1:2). In this case, he isn't telling the Corinthians to try to get sanctified or attempt to become saints, he is telling them that they already have been sanctified and are already saints because God has declared it so. God made a definite decision and declaration at some point in the past—that is, at the moment we believed—to view us and treat us as saints (or holy ones). That underemphasized aspect of sanctification is what an older man in my church calls 'a done deal.'

But what does Paul mean by saints? He doesn't mean special people in the Roman Catholic tradition (like Francis of Assisi or Mother Teresa); no, every time he addresses 'saints' in his letters he is writing to *everyone* who has accepted God's free gift of salvation through Jesus Christ. *Positional sanctification*, then, means that God has decided to view all of us who are in Christ as holy ones.

Now, here's the secret (so secret that I keep mentioning it in different ways throughout this book!): *progressive sanctification* (that is, living a life increasingly characterized by putting away sin and cultivating holy habits) is built on the foundation of *positional sanctification*. Why should a Christian strive for practical holiness, for practical and progressive sanctification? Because we were already chosen in Christ to become holy and blameless in the presence of God (Eph. 1:4); we were already redeemed from lawlessness so Christ could purify for Himself a people zealous for good works (Titus 2:14). It's time for us to learn this truth and start leaning into it. Our progress in holy living starts by understanding our position *in Christ.*

CHAPTER 40

FELLOWSHIP WITH CHRIST

> 'God is faithful, by whom you were called into the fellowship of his Son, Jesus Christ our Lord' (1 Cor. 1:9).

When I was young, I recall a youth speaker making the following claim: 'The word *fellowship* is derived from a combination of two words: "fellows" and "ship". The word "fellowship",' he declared, 'comes from a bunch of fellows on the same ship!'

Now, the idea that the word 'fellowship' in English ever had anything to do with *fellows* being on a *ship* is nonsense. Otherwise, the same ship might also carry a craftsman, a musician, a horseman, a friend, an apostle, an author, a champion, a scholar, a citizen, a partner, a governor, or a dictator, since all those words can also be combined with the suffix 'ship.' Furthermore, a group of men on a ship doesn't necessarily mean they are in fellowship. They could be at one another's throats or plotting mutiny.

'Fellowship' is actually an English translation of the Greek word *koinonia*, one of the few New Testament words familiar to many Christians. This word appears in contexts where close sharing and mutual participation are emphasized. In Paul's letters, Christians share love and unity (Phil. 2:1-2), they share communion (1 Cor. 10:16), and they share finances (Rom. 15:26; 2 Cor. 8:4). Fellowship in the sense of believer-to-believer sharing is also the idea most familiar to most modern Christians. But Paul also cared about fellowship with Christ.

The idea that a man or woman could share a close relationship with a deity who died and rose from the dead, but isn't on earth anymore, would have been viewed as preposterous by most people in the ancient world—not to mention most people I know in the modern world! But this is precisely what Paul claims. We have been called into fellowship with God's Son, Jesus Christ (1 Cor. 1:9). We haven't just been called to serve Him, though that is true. We haven't just been called to obey Him, or submit to Him, or follow Him, though all of those are also true. We have been called to be His companions… His partners… His friends.

It was my mom, who is now with the Lord, who first modeled fellowship with Christ for me. It was obvious to me as a little boy that my mom was taken with Jesus. She thought of Jesus as her friend. In fact, I can distinctly remember her saying to me as she tucked me into bed at night: 'Even if all of your friends fail you, Jesus will always be your friend. Even if you feel like you don't have a friend in the world, Jesus will always be there. He is your closest friend.' My mom understood in practice what Jesus meant when He said, 'No longer do I call you servants, for the servant does not know what his master is doing; but I have called you friends' (John 15:15). She experienced fellowship with Christ, a nearness that drew me as a boy of six to embrace Christ myself and seek fellowship with Him.

'God is faithful, by whom you were called into the fellowship of his Son, Jesus Christ our Lord' (1 Cor. 1:9). What is more important than walking in fellowship with Jesus? Let me encourage you to cultivate a daily fellowship with Jesus. When you awake in the morning, start your day by letting Him know that you love Him. As you work or study, let thoughts of Him permeate your consciousness. When you spend time with the people of God, be reminded of His loving presence. As you eat or pay bills or interact with co-workers or ride a bus, keep in mind that He wants to do these activities with you. You were called into fellowship with Christ and are able to live out that fellowship because you are *in Christ*.

CHAPTER 41

THE MIND OF CHRIST

> 'The natural person does not accept the things of the Spirit of God, for they are folly to him, and he is not able to understand them because they are spiritually discerned... "For who has understood the mind of the Lord so as to instruct him?" But we have the mind of Christ' (1 Cor. 2:14-16).

My wife and I recently celebrated a wedding anniversary on the southernmost coast of California. One day we entered a busy frozen yogurt shop on the main strip of the coastal town of Encinitas, filled our cups with our favorite flavors of frozen yogurt, added a few toppings, and headed over to pay. The teenage girl behind the counter was looking my in direction, but she didn't see me. I was only an arm's length away…and she was looking directly at me…but it never registered to her that I was standing there. I'm pretty sure she was listening to a conversation taking place behind her. As a result, I got filtered out. I cleared my throat, at which point she 'saw' me, calculated the cost, and collected my money. But when I asked for a receipt, she had already slipped back into her 'zone' and didn't even recognize that I had spoken to her! I think I held this young woman's attention for no more than eight seconds. If the police had asked her to identify me in a lineup, I'm confident that she would have said that she had never seen me before in her life!

When the Apostle Paul asserts that 'we have the mind of Christ' in 1 Corinthians 2:16, in a certain sense he is summarizing what he has already explained: that the presence of the Holy Spirit helps a believer understand and accept things about God in a way that an unbeliever cannot (1 Cor. 2:6-16). In other words, we share the perspective of Christ, mediated to us by the Holy Spirit. Unbelievers, on the other hand, are more like the teller in the frozen yogurt shop. They can look squarely at the truths about God, but still be unable to 'see' them.

Now, this passage is not saying that every thought that crosses the mind of a believer is a thought from Christ. What it is saying is that the presence of the Holy Spirit produces an enhanced perspective on the things of Christ. The Spirit reveals Christ in ways that register, impact, convict, and move toward change. An unbeliever may gaze at the same truth, but miss its significance and impact. This happens because he is absorbed with a different conversation, a conversation that distracts him from hearing the truth about God. But the spiritual person not only is enabled by the Spirit to see the truth, he is able to 'accept' it, as 1 Corinthians 2:14 suggests.

Knowing this should encourage us to cultivate sensitivity to the work of the Holy Spirit in our thinking so that we increasingly model our thoughts after those of Christ. It's not just: *what would Jesus do?* It is also: *what would Jesus think?* But it isn't even enough to ask what He *would* think; we need to be asking what Jesus *does* think. We know His thoughts in general—His overall perspective—because those thoughts have once-and-for-all been revealed in His Word; but we get help in knowing His intentions in particular situations because those intentions are highlighted and accentuated by the Holy Spirit.

As we've already observed, the 'natural person' doesn't think this way. But because Jesus sent His Spirit to His followers after He ascended to heaven, we have been given a new mind—a new way of understanding and applying the things of God—what Paul calls 'the mind of Christ.' We have this renewed mind, a new way of thinking, because we are *in Christ*.

CHAPTER 42

SEXUAL PURITY IN CHRIST

'"Food is meant for the stomach and the stomach for food"—and God will destroy both one and the other. The body is not meant for sexual immorality, but for the Lord, and the Lord for the body... Do you not know that your bodies are members of Christ? Shall I then take the members of Christ and make them members of a prostitute? Never! Or do you not know that he who is joined to a prostitute becomes one body with her? For, as it is written, "The two will become one flesh." But he who is joined to the Lord becomes one spirit with him' (1 Cor. 6:13-17).

Your sexuality doesn't define you. Are you tempted to sin with members of the opposite sex? As a believer in Christ, you are not defined by those desires. Do you feel same-sex attractions? Such desires don't define you, either. You are no more defined by your sexual desires than you are, say, by your desire to drink coffee. Your cravings for coffee may be insistent and strong; indeed, for many the impulse is compulsive. But just because 'food is meant for the stomach and the stomach for food,' doesn't mean that who you are is defined by your urge to eat—or drink coffee. But if desire doesn't define you, what does?

1 Corinthians 6:13-17 cries out a resounding answer to that question: If you are *in Christ* you are defined by *that*. 'Your bodies are members of Christ' (v. 15). You are 'joined to the Lord' and become 'one spirit with him' (v. 17). The Apostle Paul exhorts you to pursue sexual purity on the basis of your *inChristness*. There's more to say

about winning the battle for sexual purity, but learning the importance of your union with Christ is foundational to everything else.

Both sets of parents of a young couple I know insist that the couple joins them every year for Thanksgiving dinner. For whatever reason, the young couple has not yet been able to negotiate their way toward a resolution of this dilemma, so every year they attend *two* Thanksgiving meals. Mid-afternoon on Thanksgiving Day they partake in the first family meal—turkey, stuffing, mashed potatoes, gravy, yams, cranberry sauce…finishing it off with pumpkin pie. Then they graciously bid farewell, drive down the road, and sit down to another *huge* Thanksgiving dinner of turkey, stuffing, mashed potatoes…

How strong do you think is their desire to eat the second meal? Not strong at all. In fact, the thought of sitting down to a second Thanksgiving feast repulses them. No matter how carefully they eat during their first meal, they *never* feel hungry when they arrive at the second.

So it is for those who deeply embrace their *inChristness* instead of caving into their sexual cravings. Those who are *full* of Christ don't desire something more than Christ. Multiple slices of pumpkin pie topped with whipped cream later in the day won't entice them. In the sex-saturated age in which we live, the only people who consistently overcome in the battle for sexual purity are those who are so full of Christ that their desire for sexual sin is minimal compared to their desire to live their lives wholly *in Christ*. Your desire to sin will decrease as you are filled with the life of Christ.

With this truth utterly and wholeheartedly embraced, we can then address the practicalities of the battle for sexual purity: developing godly habits, avoiding places of temptation, exposing the roots of our urges, cultivating godly friendships to talk about temptation, and fleeing sin in the moment of temptation. But the driving desire for sexual sin will diminish as we learn, lean into, and live out the truth that we are already full if we are *in Christ*.

CHAPTER 43

IMITATORS OF CHRIST

> 'Be imitators of me, as I am of Christ' (1 Cor. 11:1).
>
> 'And you became imitators of us and of the Lord' (1 Thess. 1:6).
>
> 'Therefore be imitators of God, as beloved children. And walk in love, as Christ loved us and gave himself up for us, a fragrant offering and sacrifice to God' (Eph. 5:1-2).

One of the best-known pieces of Christian devotional literature ever written is *The Imitation of Christ* by Thomas à Kempis. His little book—originally written in Latin—has been translated into multiple languages and republished hundreds of times since its composition in the early fifteenth century. John Wesley in the eighteenth century thought so highly of the book that he translated it into English. The book includes various pieces of wise counsel on the nature and exercise of humility, the benefits of solitude and silence, and how to approach suffering. Some have criticized the book, and perhaps rightly so, for its seeming disengagement from regular life. But many Christians have found its spiritual guidance helpful even while acknowledging that it has a few blind spots endemic to the age in which it was written.

But there is one serious shortcoming of this book I have never heard anyone mention. The lack of emphasis on union with Christ in *The Imitation of Christ* means that the author of this little book sometimes puts his emphasis in the wrong place. The author, like so many before him—not to mention so many more in our generation—focuses on the 'how to's' of Christian living, and thereby hinders his readers from adequately engaging with the fount of Christian living: *inChristness*.

It is true that Paul calls us to imitate Christ. But Paul's instructions must be understood in the context of everything else he has written about *inChristness*. We indeed are called to look to Christ as our example (1 Cor. 11:1; 1 Thess. 1:6), we should seek to walk in love by observing Christ's own sacrificial love (Eph. 5:2), and we learn the nature of humility by looking to Christ (Phil. 2:5). But ours is not an imitation that comes from peering at Christ from a distance and trying to copy Him; ours is an imitation flowing out of an inextricable and intimate connection to Christ.

My dad recently told me a story from my childhood that may illustrate this. He recounted a day I asked him to help me move a box that was too heavy for me to lift. Dad told me that he walked over to the box and started to pick it up on his own, but then thought better of it. He turned to me and said, 'You asked me to help you. So let's pick it up together.' Even though he could have picked up the box himself, he invited me to join him, and so allowed me the privilege of doing it together with him.

My dad showed me how to pick up the box; indeed, he was my example of how to do it. But he did not leave me to pick it up on my own, something I couldn't have done anyway. I moved the box *with him.* It is only because we have been united with Christ that we can ever hope to serve as Christ served, forgive as Christ forgave, and love as Christ loved. By all means, open the Gospels and seek to emulate the example of Jesus. But never forget that our imitation of Christ doesn't occur as we contemplate Him from a distance and then try hard to work it out on our own. Imitation of Christ flows out of an intimate relationship with Christ. We have been invited to imitate Christ because we are already *in Christ.*

CHAPTER 44

HOPE IN CHRIST

'If in Christ we have hope in this life only, we are of all people most to be pitied' (1 Cor. 15:19).

'Christ in you, the hope of glory' (Col. 1:27).

'remembering before our God and Father your... steadfastness of hope in our Lord Jesus Christ' (1 Thess. 1:3).

'Christ Jesus our hope' (1 Tim. 1:1).

What do you anticipate most when you think about heaven?

I look forward to the end of all sin and suffering, tears and tragedy, war and weeping. I look forward to meeting angels who have fought epic battles in the heavenlies and quietly ministered to me during my time on earth. I look forward to the opportunity to thank saints from the past who have endured suffering, pursued holiness, and modeled for me how to walk the road of faith. I look forward to being reunited with my mom. I look forward to eating good food, entering into deeply meaningful worship, experiencing a new creation not marred by the fall, and embarking on whatever future service God has prepared for me. But most of all, I look forward to being with Jesus. I long to be in the presence of the One I have come to love more than life itself. My hope is *in* Christ. Actually, my hope *is* Christ.

But 'hope' is such a weak word in English, isn't it? We say things like, 'I hope she falls in love with me,' even if there's little evidence she knows you even exist, or 'I hope a lot of people come to my party tonight,' even when we suspect few will actually show up, or even 'I hope my teacher will change my exam grade,' although there is little hope of that at all!

But biblical hope isn't weak; it brims with anticipation. Hope is the fervent expectation of what is coming in the future based upon the integrity of the One who has promised to accomplish it. Biblical hope is not wishing that Jesus would come back soon; it is confidence that Jesus is going to return, make everything right, and take us to be with Him in His eternal kingdom. It is rooted and grounded in Christ's promise, guaranteed by His trustworthiness, and sealed by the Holy Spirit. Our hope is in Christ. Another way of viewing it—as the Apostle Paul himself views it—is that Jesus Himself *is* our hope. We should view Christ not only as the One who made the promise, or as the One who provides the way, or as the One who will bring to completion all that He promised—even though all that is true. He Himself is the very thing for which we hope (Col. 1:27; 1 Thess. 1:3; 1 Tim. 1:1).

I have been hoping—intensely longing—to be with Christ ever since I was a fourteen-year-old high school freshman. That's when God truly captured my heart. One night I started thinking about the length of eternity compared to the brevity of life. I lost sleep over it—lots of sleep. That was the best loss of sleep I ever experienced! I still think a lot about the incredible future that God has prepared for me. I have *never* gotten over what God started in me when I was fourteen.

When I hear a Christian say, 'I've lost hope,' I want to shout: 'Your hope is not based upon whether you have feelings of hope! Your hope is *in Christ* with whom you have been united, who lives within you, who has promised and prepared a splendid future for you, who is Himself your hope of glory!'

Dear Christian, you will discover so much courage in your spiritual journey by cultivating a focused anticipation of the glorious future that Christ has prepared for you. You can hope to be with Christ knowing that you are already *in Christ*.

CHAPTER 45

SHARING CHRIST'S SUFFERINGS

'we share abundantly in Christ's sufferings' (2 Cor. 1:5).

'For it has been granted to you that for the sake of Christ you should not only believe in him but also suffer for his sake' (Phil. 1:29).

'that I may know him...and may share his sufferings' (Phil. 3:10).

There is a line in a well-known story of Jesus (Matt. 20:20-28) that often gets overlooked. James and John have just allowed their *mommy* to ask Jesus for permission for them to sit at His right and left hand in His coming kingdom. Jesus ignores the mother and speaks to the two men: 'You do not know what you are asking. Are you able to drink the cup that I am to drink?'

They (foolishly) reply, 'We are able.'

Jesus counters, 'You will drink my cup, but to sit at my right hand and at my left is not mine to grant, but it is for those for whom it has been prepared by my Father.'

The story continues as the other ten disciples get upset with the two brothers, setting the stage for a powerful lesson by Jesus on servanthood, which is the main point of the recorded dialogue.

But did you pick up what Jesus told the disciples? Jesus predicted that *they would drink His cup*! This statement takes your breath away when you recall that at the Last Supper Jesus symbolized the blood that would pour from His own body with a *cup* of wine (Matt. 26:27-29), at Gethsemane Jesus agonized that the *cup* of suffering might be removed from Him (Matt. 26:37-39), and at His arrest Jesus told Peter to put away his sword, adding: 'shall I not drink the *cup* that the Father has given me?' (John 18:11).

Let me anticipate a question that might have already entered your mind: Wasn't Jesus's suffering unique—something only He could do? Yes, Jesus's cup of suffering on the cross was unique; only His death could provide substitutionary atonement for our sins. That may be why Jesus rebuked the arrogance of James and John who thoughtlessly supposed they could drink His cup.

But there's more to say. Jesus invites every disciple into suffering; there is a cup of suffering every disciple must drink. 'A servant is not greater than his master' (John 15:20). Servants suffer along with their master.

So when the Apostle Paul reminds us that we share in Christ's sufferings (2 Cor. 1:5; Phil. 1:29; 3:10), he's just repeating what Jesus taught earlier. We shouldn't expect our lives to be free of suffering, whether the kind we face when someone doesn't like that we're Christians, or the common kind of pain or disease that everyone in a fallen and broken world experiences. If somehow you started your Christian life without someone explaining that you were signing up for suffering, it's time to break it to you: there is no such thing as a Christian life without suffering.

But I find Paul's honesty strangely comforting. He is not trying to hide the truth. When my wife and I lived in the Middle East, an elderly man—wise and godly—met with some of us who were serving the Lord there. One evening he cautiously reminded us that our decision to live as ambassadors for Christ in a difficult part of the world could place our long-term mental health at risk (not to mention other kinds of health). His words helped, since they validated what we had already begun to observe and experience. But isn't Jesus worth even that? Thanks be to Jesus—we don't suffer alone! We *share* in His sufferings. He walks with us through our suffering. He is with us in *our* sufferings because we are connected to Him in *His* sufferings. Sharing Christ's sufferings is one more aspect of what it means to be *in Christ*.

CHAPTER 46

COMFORT IN CHRIST

> 'For as we share abundantly in Christ's sufferings, so through Christ we share abundantly in comfort too' (2 Cor. 1:5).
>
> 'So if there is any encouragement in Christ, any comfort from love' (Phil. 2:1).

I often call my wife after something difficult happens at work.

The daughter of a powerful New York City lawyer publicly threatened to sue my college—and me personally—because I wouldn't allow her to take an exam on her own timetable and terms. After I calmed down a bit, I called Trudi. Years later, two of my students in Southern California nearly got into a fistfight during a Greek class. Afterward, I called Trudi. Then there was the day I discovered that a student had figured out a way to manipulate his course grade. I called Trudi that day as well.

There is comfort in connection, and what connection is closer than being *in Christ*? The Apostle Paul writes, 'For as we share abundantly in Christ's sufferings, so through Christ we share abundantly in comfort too' (2 Cor. 1:5).

Why is it that when I have a bad dream I reach over to touch my wife? I don't even have to wake her up to experience comfort from her presence. But there are real ways in which Christ is closer than my wife.

The suffering that Paul wrote about in the first chapter of 2 Corinthians was a lot worse than an altercation with a student in a classroom or a frightening dream. Paul's language was downright dark when he described the 'affliction in Asia' that he and his co-workers experienced. 'Utterly burdened'... 'beyond our strength'... 'we despaired even of life itself.' He called it a 'deadly peril' and painfully recalled that it was like receiving 'the sentence of death' (2 Cor. 1:8-10). No one knows for sure what Paul and his colleagues faced in Asia Minor, but whatever it was, it was excruciating.

Despite their horrific ordeal, Paul and his coworkers found comfort in Christ. The Greek word, *paraklesis*, is the most important word in the passage, appearing in one form or another nine times in 2 Corinthians 1:3-7. Still, I'm a bit surprised that almost every English translation uses the word 'comfort' to translate this Greek word. It's certainly an acceptable translation since 'comfort' is a common-enough meaning of this word, and 'comfort' fits the context well enough. But I still think something has been lost in translation. You see, it isn't simply that Paul and his coworkers were soothed by God in the midst of their sufferings, as 'comfort' might imply. Paul is saying that they received spiritual *strengthening* and *encouragement* by God, which allowed them to persevere through trials. The most common translation of this Greek word in other places in the New Testament is not 'comfort,' but 'encouragement,' like the first noun in Philippians 2:1: 'So if there is any encouragement in Christ…' (Interestingly, even the English word 'comfort' used to mean something closer to internal *strengthening*; compare the Old French word *conforter* and the Late Latin word *confortare*.[16]) Second Corinthians 1:3-7 not only teaches that God comforts us in our affliction, it communicates that He spiritually strengthens us and encourages us when we suffer in Christ.

A small child claims to be afraid of the dark. His mom asks him, 'If I were to turn off the light right now, would you be afraid?' 'No, you're here with me.' 'Then you're not afraid of the dark,' replies his mom wisely, 'you're afraid of being alone in the dark.'

Being *in Christ* entails that we are never alone. We are constantly connected to Jesus. We need never fear the dark, no matter how dark it gets. God's comfort—and indeed, spiritual strengthening and encouragement—is one of God's most precious gifts for those who are *in Christ*.

CHAPTER 47

GLORY OF CHRIST

'As for Titus, he is my partner and fellow worker for your benefit. And as for our brothers, they are messengers of the churches, the glory of Christ' (2 Cor. 8:23).

'so that the name of our Lord Jesus may be glorified in you, and you in him, according to the grace of our God and the Lord Jesus Christ' (2 Thess. 1:12).

'To this he called you through our gospel, so that you may obtain the glory of our Lord Jesus Christ' (2 Thess. 2:14).

Paul wasn't a loner, despite persistent rumors to the contrary. People frequently view Paul as a driven and ambitious missionary who launched out on his own to carry the good news to yet unreached regions. But Paul was not a loner. Paul is almost always portrayed in the Bible as traveling with and ministering alongside *others*. In fact, in the only two moments in Paul's letters where he mentions being alone, he seems rather unhappy about it (1 Thess. 3:1; 2 Tim. 4:11).

An example of Paul's group orientation is found in 2 Corinthians 8:16-24. In those verses he mentions Titus (one of Paul's closest mentees), as well as some Christian brother he decides to leave unnamed (if you want a good historical puzzle, try to figure out who the 'brother' of 8:22 is!), and lets us know that there were others with him as well (8:23). These men were probably traveling with Paul for two reasons: (1) they were honest, and (2) they were strong—no one was gonna' mess with them! Paul needed travelling companions at this point in his ministry because he was transporting a large sum of money he had collected from the Gentile churches to the impoverished believers in Jerusalem. The Gentile churches had appointed men to travel with him to make sure the money got distributed as intended—and so that no thieves would try to hoist it along the way.

But, strikingly, Paul refers to this group of burly guys as 'the glory of Christ' (2 Cor. 8:23). Which means that Paul had noticed that their character, demeanor, and actions radiated Christ!

What does it mean for a person to be the *glory* of Christ? Or, similarly, what does Paul mean in 2 Thessalonians 1:12 when he writes: 'so that the name of our Lord Jesus may be glorified in you, and you in him'?

It means that the honor that Jesus already possesses gets publicized when *in-Christ* people live in a manner that others can observe and recognize that they are connected to Jesus. The words 'glory' and 'name' are words that had a richer significance for first-century Mediterranean persons than they have for most of us. All the people reading Paul's letters lived in cultures where the pursuit of honor and avoidance of shame was a central cultural value. So if someone got described as *the glory of someone else*, this meant that person #1 increased the social honor of person #2 because person #1 was connected to person #2 and acted in ways that reflected well on person #2. So if someone referred to a son as the glory of his father, this meant that the son publicly brought honor to his father through the way he lived. And conversely, if the father receives glory, then the son does too.

Do you want people to give honor to your precious Lord Jesus when they observe your manner of life? Then live life—as did those brawny guys who traveled with Paul to Jerusalem—in such a way that the name of Jesus gets glorified through you. Then you, too, might get called 'the glory of Christ.' Wouldn't that be something! May God receive all the glory and honor in you and through you as you live your life *in Christ.*

CHAPTER 48

THOUGHT-LIFE IN CHRIST

> 'We destroy arguments and every lofty opinion raised against the knowledge of God, and take every thought captive to obey Christ' (2 Cor. 10:5).

Joaquín Guzmán, better known to the world as El Chapo ('shorty'), was a Mexican drug lord who wielded extensive power and committed terrible crimes as the leader of a cartel he led. But he is perhaps best known as the guy who kept getting away. He eluded police and military personnel on multiple occasions when they tried to arrest him, and even twice escaped from maximum-security federal prisons.

El Chapo is like our thought lives. It's a strange analogy, I know, but it's one Paul utilizes. Paul suggests the analogy of an elusive prisoner who keeps trying to break away to describe the tendencies of our thoughts. We try to 'take every thought captive to obey Christ' (2 Cor. 10:5), but somehow our thoughts keep breaking out of jail.

Think about it. Even during worship services when everything is designed to focus on God—music, message, testimonies—sometimes we find our minds not only wandering, but even wandering into areas that don't honor God.

What can we do about our jail-breaking thoughts? Our minds wander so easily. What do we need to do in order to take every thought captive to obey Christ? Here are six suggestions:

1. Be honest about how often you allow your thoughts to wander. Confess to the Lord your need for Him to help you with your wayward thoughts.

2. Remind yourself of gospel truth. One of my friends from many years ago often reminded me to keep preaching the gospel to myself! That's a good word. Challenge your own wrong thoughts about the

character of God whenever they cross your mind (…that He isn't concerned about holiness…that He doesn't actually love you…that He doesn't care about your problems), and constantly remind yourself of the substitutionary sacrifice of Christ on your behalf.

3. Keep bringing to mind not just general biblical truth, but specific Scriptures you have memorized. Paragraphs are better than individual verses (and whole chapters and books are better than paragraphs), but keep reciting whatever Scripture you know. Of course, this assumes that you have at least some Scripture memorized…

4. Fill your thinking with prayer. By constantly talking to God, your thoughts will have neither the time nor the desire to jailbreak.

5. Lessen your media input. Put the brakes on the thousands of messages that keep bombarding your mind. Watch less television; look at your phone and computer screen less frequently than you typically do.

6. Remember to connect your thought-life to your *inChristness*. Here are a few examples:

When you start to despair, and start thinking that no one cares about you or that God isn't interested in you, remember that the Lord Jesus is always with you and always cares. When you are tempted to pursue something merely to gratify your flesh, remember that Jesus suffered in the flesh for you and that your body belongs to Him. When you start to believe the lie that Jesus cannot handle your problems, remember that Jesus took on humanity, identified with your suffering, and has invited you into a new life with Him. When you start focusing on yourself, or begin seeking your own pleasure, remember that Christ *is* your life. When you begin to desire the property or lifestyle of another, remember that all the spiritual riches in the world are yours because you belong to Christ.

If you are already in Christ, then nothing in heaven or earth can separate you from that connection. Constantly think about the truths that connect to that reality. Let such thoughts be at the forefront of your mind.

Don't let your thoughts jailbreak. Focus instead on the truth that you are *in Christ*.

CHAPTER 49

SINCERE DEVOTION TO CHRIST

> 'But I am afraid that as the serpent deceived Eve by his cunning, your thoughts will be led astray from a sincere and pure devotion to Christ' (2 Cor. 11:3).

A daily verse. Just one Bible verse on which to focus throughout the day. Do you sometimes come across a verse that you know will be of help to you in your spiritual life, commit it to memory, and then keep repeating that verse to yourself throughout the day? I have used 2 Corinthians 11:3 in such a manner many times. Why this verse in particular? Because I know how easily I get distracted, sidetracked, and tempted to subtly shift my focus away from devotion to Christ. Some things that shift my focus are good things. But when they shift the center, life is out of focus. So I preach a warning to myself again and again using 2 Corinthians 11:3: 'Ken, I am afraid that as the serpent deceived Eve by his cunning, your thoughts will be led astray from a sincere and pure devotion to Christ.'

But what about the seventy emails I need to read because they backed up while I was out of town? Shouldn't I just sit down and plow through them?

I am afraid that as the serpent deceived Eve by his cunning, your thoughts will be led astray from a sincere and pure devotion to Christ.

Still, I have to get this project done. If it's not finished on time, my supervisors and colleagues are going to be disappointed in me.

I am afraid that as the serpent deceived Eve by his cunning, your thoughts will be led astray from a sincere and pure devotion to Christ.

But my kids... I know they are a gift from God, and...I'm exceedingly grateful for them. But I'm so tired! Their needs are unending, their desires insatiable, and my ability too meager for what is required.

I am afraid that as the serpent deceived Eve by his cunning, your thoughts will be led astray from a sincere and pure devotion to Christ.

He used to be one of my best friends. I can't think of anything else I can do to soften the tension between us. I long to be reconciled, but he doesn't want anything to do with me anymore. I can't stop thinking about it.

I am afraid that as the serpent deceived Eve by his cunning, your thoughts will be led astray from a sincere and pure devotion to Christ.

I'm worried that my reputation will be ruined.

I am afraid that as the serpent deceived Eve by his cunning, your thoughts will be led astray from a sincere and pure devotion to Christ.

A lot of people are counting on me.

I am afraid that as the serpent deceived Eve by his cunning, your thoughts will be led astray from a sincere and pure devotion to Christ.

I have so many things to do today.

I am afraid that as the serpent deceived Eve by his cunning, your thoughts will be led astray from a sincere and pure devotion to Christ.

'Lord, I acknowledge my lack of focus—that my devotion is less than sincere. I know deep down that it's not about my attempts to succeed, or what others think of me, or whether I feel good about myself. I am connected to you; that's what ultimately matters more than anything else. I long to express sincere and pure devotion to you. I know that such devotion doesn't just happen—or even come about by simply trying hard to obtain it. I am in you, Lord Jesus Christ, and the source of my devotion is you.'

My devotion is grounded in the reality that I am *in Christ*.

CHAPTER 50

WEAKNESS AND POWER IN CHRIST

> 'But he said to me, "My grace is sufficient for you, for my power is made perfect in weakness." Therefore I will boast all the more gladly of my weaknesses, so that the power of Christ may rest upon me' (2 Cor. 12:9).

It was the most excruciating pain I had ever felt. Far more painful than lower back spasms, and even worse than shingles—the two most intense pains I had previously encountered. The doctors called it trigeminal neuralgia, which is defined as stabbing nerve pain on one side of the face. A string of doctors were in agreement that this terrible pain, striking my face in short, intense, and unexpected intervals, might be my companion for life.

I received my diagnosis almost two years ago as I write this. During the first two months, the pain was, honestly, so severe that I thought life as I knew it was over. Unless something changed, it was clear to me that I would never again be able to teach, preach, or even engage in regular conversations without interruptions from uncontrollable pain. Thankfully, a researcher some time ago noticed that a couple of anti-seizure medicines can somewhat mitigate this kind of pain, at least for a while. Now, almost two years later, things are mostly under control, although break-out pain on the right side of my face still occurs dozens of times a week, though, thankfully, not nearly at the same levels I experienced when the ordeal started. I can still teach at the university, even though I have to forewarn my students at the beginning of each semester that I might experience a painful episode in the middle of a lesson, just so they don't freak out.

Actually, this is one of the final chapters I am writing in this book. (I didn't write all the chapters in order.) I was about halfway through the book when this painful condition started. The spiritual help I have received from meditating on the great doctrinal and practical implications of being *in Christ* during a season of pain has been immense.

But of all the in-Christ passages I have encountered while writing this book, I have received more encouragement from meditating on 2 Corinthians 12:7-10 than from any other. The Apostle Paul encountered some sort of stabbing (literal? metaphorical?) pain—what he referred to as his 'thorn in the flesh' (2 Cor. 12:7).[17] He implored the Lord three times to take it away. But the Lord spoke profound words that have deeply ministered to me: 'My grace is sufficient for you, for my power is made perfect in weakness' (2 Cor. 12:9). The truths in this compelling sentence will sustain you, too, if you continually recall that you are *in Christ* despite your pain. The connection between weakness, power, and *inChristness* gets underscored by Paul in the very next chapter when he writes: 'we also are weak *in him*,' but 'we will live *with him*' by the power of God' (2 Cor. 13:4).

But how is power perfected in weakness, someone might ask? Let me suggest that the process begins when we start believing the truth that unless God acts, we are unable to make any spiritual impact, change or grow in any way, or come to know the power of God to any degree. We have to arrive at a place where we truly and clearly understand that we are *weak*. One of the primary means God uses to teach this lesson is pain. He allows pain in our lives to lead us into a recognition of our weakness, so that we can learn to depend solely upon Him. This opens the door to God working His power in and through our lives. Our weakness, suffering, and pain as people *in Christ,* unexpectedly, leads to spiritual power *in Christ.*

CHAPTER 51

PLEASING CHRIST

> 'So whether we are at home or away, we make it our aim to please him' (2 Cor. 5:9).
>
> 'Am I now trying to gain the approval of people, or of God? Or am I trying to please people? If I were still trying to please people, I would not be a slave of Christ!' (Gal. 1:10 NET).
>
> 'and try to discern what is pleasing to the Lord' (Eph. 5:10).

Are you a people-pleaser? Do you do things for others so they will like you, thank you, or just not get upset at you?

The Urban Dictionary facetiously remarks that when people-pleasers die, it isn't their own lives that flash before their eyes; they see the life of someone else flash before their eyes![18]

There is a well-known parable in the Middle East of a father who sets his young son on a donkey as they travel together toward town. As they journey they overhear some folks on the side of the road complain that the boy has no respect for his father. So the son asks his father to allow him to walk while his father rides the donkey. But no sooner have the two changed places than they overhear someone criticizing the father for making his son walk while the father rides. So the father and son together mount the donkey. But as you may have guessed, yet someone else censures them for overburdening the poor beast. In one version of the story, the father and son—in an exasperated attempt to please people—try to pick up the donkey and end up falling into the river!

Where did this expression 'people-pleaser' come from anyway? I don't know for sure, but perhaps the Apostle Paul had something to do with it. Paul writes, 'Or am I trying to please people? If I were still trying to please people, I would not be a slave of Christ' (Gal. 1:10 NET). Take note of the contrast Paul draws here. *Either* he is serving Christ, *or* he is a people-pleaser. Our life-orientation cannot be focused on trying to please people if we want to be servants of Christ.

But this is where it gets tricky. Serving others in love is something every Christian is called to do (Gal. 5:13). People-pleasers serve others. And people who get served by people-pleasers often appreciate receiving the service. So what's the difference between being a people-pleaser and serving out of love? The main difference is *motive*. Why do you do what you do? Where is your heart in service? Do you crave the approval of others? Are you driven by a desire for people to like you? Or, are you motivated by the desire to serve God when you serve others?

Why did you stay up late to finish that particular project even though you were already short on sleep? Was it because you genuinely thought that the Lord would be pleased that you sacrificed sleep to serve another? If so, your loss of sleep was worth it. Or was your primary motive that you didn't want someone to be disappointed in you? Be honest. Your answer will help you determine whether you tend toward being a God-pleaser or a people-pleaser.

If you discover that you gravitate toward people-pleasing, confess it openly to the Lord. Start reminding yourself that if you are *in Christ*, then your most important audience is Christ. And don't stop reminding yourself. Bring this truth to mind over and over again. You are not hostage to others' opinions. You belong to Someone else. Your service should be motivated by your central focus on Christ. You don't have to be a people-pleaser anymore because you are *in Christ*.

CHAPTER 52

FAITH IN CHRIST

'I live by faith in the Son of God, who loved me and gave himself for me' (Gal. 2:20).

'I have heard of your faith in the Lord Jesus and your love toward all the saints' (Eph. 1:15).

'so that Christ may dwell in your hearts through faith' (Eph. 3:17).

'rejoicing to see your good order and the firmness of your faith in Christ' (Col. 2:5).

In recent years, the cultural gatekeepers of movies and popular music have released numerous films and songs that promote faith. In fact, I just finished searching the words 'just believe' at a song lyrics site. Here are today's results: 'We've found *40,410* lyrics, *16* artists, and *100* albums matching "just believe".'

Of course, the faith being promoted by our media outlets is either empty faith (faith in faith) or faith in oneself; it bears little resemblance to biblical faith. I sincerely hope that your understanding of faith hasn't been overly influenced by such messages, though I have to believe (excuse the pun) that it has for some of us reading this chapter. So what is faith, really?

Faith is relying on Christ's faithfulness. It is trusting in the trustworthiness of Christ. It is dependence on Christ's dependability. In other words, faith—true faith—is intrinsically tied to being *in Christ*. It isn't *just believing* (wishful thinking that maybe something will happen). It certainly isn't believing in yourself.

Faith is commonly linked with the words 'in Christ' in the letters of Paul. Since my goal in this book is to elucidate how Paul applies the doctrine of union with Christ (*inChristness*) to life, it is worth highlighting that the connection of *inChristness* with faith is one common way Paul understands our connection with Christ making a difference in our lives. There are two ways he does it.

First, Paul sometimes uses 'faith in Christ' (or similar expressions) to mean believing in Christ as the means by which we as sinful people are made right in the sight of a holy God. In theological language, this is faith in Christ for justification (Gal. 2:16; 3:22-26; Rom. 3:22, 26; Phil. 3:9; 1 Tim. 1:16; 2 Tim. 3:15).

The second way Paul writes about 'faith in Christ' has to do with sanctification, or our daily growth toward holiness (Gal. 2:20; Eph. 1:15; 3:17; Col. 2:5). This sort of faith is the daily entrusting of ourselves to God's plans in dependence, surrender, and yieldedness. This kind of faith is the focus of our reflection in this chapter.

But I fear that the language of faith has been so diluted in the popular media that we might still struggle to know what faith-in-practice looks like. So let me offer a few examples.

Faith is receiving a diagnosis that you have a potentially painful and debilitating condition for which there is no cure, but refusing to look away from Christ because you trust His faithfulness to see you through. Faith is viewing the Lord as your master and seeking to do your work well even though you feel overworked, underpaid, and underappreciated by your employer. Faith is stepping into a new ministry—even one that may feel beyond your capacity—because you have learned to depend upon Christ's proven dependability. Faith is leaning into the truth that you are *in Christ* and that nothing can dislodge you from that truth even when someone mocks your ethnicity, your family, your education, your social status, or your commitment to the Word of God. Faith is continuing to pray, even though you've been praying for a long time with no response, because you believe that the prayer you offer is a Christ-honoring prayer.

Faith is not faith in faith (whatever that means!), nor is it faith in oneself; true faith has always been and always will be faith *in Christ*.

CHAPTER 53

FORMATION IN CHRIST

> 'my little children, for whom I am again in the anguish of childbirth until Christ is formed in you!' (Gal. 4:19).

Have you come across the term 'spiritual formation'? If yes, have you wondered where in the Bible the term comes from? One source may be Galatians 4:19, '…until Christ is *formed* in you' (Rom. 8:29 and 12:2 are also possible sources). 'Spiritual formation' is a modern catch-phrase for what earlier generations referred to as Christian living, spiritual growth, discipleship to Christ, or sanctification. 'Formation' actually is a good way of describing God's goal for us, and Galatians 4:19 offers a few hints about how we should understand the process.

There are four things to notice about Galatians 4:19 in its context: (1) God is the One who forms the believer, (2) the person being formed should cooperate with what God is doing, (3) other Christians can play supportive roles, and (4) childbirth is a good analogy to explain the process.

The first and most important thing to get from this passage is that you cannot spiritually form yourself. In the childbirth analogy, you are the child to be formed while God is the One who forms you. God grows and shapes a baby in the womb. Neither is the process accomplished partly by God and partly by you. In the same way, as you are spiritually formed, God gets all the credit, since apart from Him you could never be formed in Christ.

Second, we need to cooperate with what God seeks to do in us. Even though He is responsible for forming us, we need to receive His formational work and properly respond to His initiative. The alternative is to obstruct or slow down the work of God in our lives through legalism, lethargy, or lack of faith, to offer a few examples. The

Galatians, as a negative example, had allowed false teachers to propagate a law-centered version of the Christian life, and thereby impeded some of the transformational work God had already started in them.

Other Christians can play a positive role in God's process of forming us in Christ. In the childbirth analogy, Paul was the Galatians' midwife who ushered them into a new life, and he certainly didn't want to repeat the process! His passion for the Galatians led him to pray for them constantly (he often prayed for far-away Christians, Rom. 1:10; Eph. 1:16; 1 Thess. 1:2). Furthermore, his attempt to protect them from Judaizing teachers is one of the ways God used him to guard the Galatian Christians so nothing would get in the way of their growth. God sometimes uses other believers to protect and help during the process of Christian formation.

How long does the process take? Paul says his labor continues 'until Christ is formed in you.' The change occurs little bits at a time over the course of a Christian's life.

Progressively, the Christ-life, including Christ's motivations and values, becomes so much a part of your own life that when people look at you, they see Jesus in you more and more each day. They increasingly observe evidences of grace, humility, love, boldness, faith, and the like, and so begin to turn their thoughts toward Jesus whenever they encounter you.

So, brothers and sisters, let's cooperate with what God wants to do in us. Let's not act like some of the Galatian Christians who were led astray into thinking that they somehow were better Christians by adding particular (in their case, Jewish) practices to the righteous standing that they already possessed through their *inChristness*. Nor let us in any other way resist the formational work that God seeks to do in us. For, you see, the basis and starting point for all spiritual formation isn't what we do, but is the work that God has done. All spiritual formation is *in Christ*.

CHAPTER 54

THANKFULNESS IN CHRIST

> 'Blessed be the God and Father of our Lord Jesus Christ... to the praise of his glorious grace...so that we who were the first to hope in Christ might be to the praise of his glory' (Eph. 1:3, 6, 12).
>
> 'And whatever you do, in word or deed, do everything in the name of the Lord Jesus, giving thanks to God the Father through him' (Col. 3:17).
>
> 'give thanks in all circumstances; for this is the will of God in Christ Jesus for you' (1 Thess. 5:18).

Thanksgiving in the United States is one of my favorite holidays. I used to view it as the only religious holiday still untainted by secularism and materialism. But that was before football took over. Now, for many of us, largely because of the national obsession with American-style football, the most thanks that gets expressed on our day of *thanksgiving* is a brief prayer offered before we inhale a magnificent spread of turkey and stuffing (brief, so people can get back to watching the game!). Of course, there is a type of thanksgiving expressed—loudly and with whoops of joy—when a favorite football team wins a game, though such thanksgiving is not (usually) expressed to God. Ironically, our exuberant thankfulness at our favorite sports team's success may be closer to the level of exuberance expressed by the Apostle Paul (in places like Ephesians 1) than are the words of thanks many of us utter during our pre-turkey prayer.

But thanksgiving in Christ is *way* more than a short thanking of God for a meal or a favorite team's victory. Thanksgiving in the letters of Paul is one way of describing *the entire Christian life*. This is not an exaggeration. One simple way to describe the Christian life is this: God showed us grace, and our response to that grace should be a life lived out of gratitude. Paul put it like this: 'And whatever you do, in word or deed, do everything in the name of the Lord Jesus, giving thanks to God the Father through him' (Col. 3:17). This gratitude-in-all-of-life impacts numerous aspects of Christian living.

The manner in which we serve illustrates the point well. Christian service isn't simply making a decision to serve, and then 'gritting out' our service. We perform acts of service in conscious awareness of the lavish grace we have received from God! God looked upon us, criminals ('sinners') that we were, and chose to send Jesus to die in our place. As a response, we sacrificially serve others because we have received unbounded grace.

The sinful woman who poured expensive ointment on Jesus's feet and wiped His feet with her hair illustrates the relationship between thankfulness and service. When Simon the Pharisee complained (in his own head) that Jesus shouldn't have allowed a sinful woman to touch Him, Jesus challenged those thoughts with: 'he who is forgiven little, loves little' (Luke 7:47). But the woman at Jesus's feet knew how much she had been forgiven, then allowed that grace to move her heart toward thankfulness, and the result was an extravagant act of service to Jesus.

Did you know that Abraham Lincoln issued his two famous Thanksgiving proclamations (proclamations 106 and 118) in 1863 and 1864 respectively—*before* the end of the American Civil War? Lincoln recognized that thanksgiving should not only be expressed when things were bright, but was vital during dark and dangerous days as well. Paul said that we should 'give thanks in all circumstances; for this is the will of God in Christ Jesus for you' (1 Thess 5:18). We need to live all of life with an attitude of thanksgiving for God's grace to us in Christ Jesus whether life is relatively easy or desperately hard.

The Christian life is simply a life filled with thankfulness for what God has done *in Christ*.

CHAPTER 55

GROWTH AND MATURITY IN CHRIST

> 'until we all attain to the unity of the faith and of the knowledge of the Son of God, to mature manhood, to the measure of the stature of the fullness of Christ so that we may no longer be children, tossed to and fro by the waves and carried about by every wind of doctrine, by human cunning, by craftiness in deceitful schemes. Rather, speaking the truth in love, we are to grow up in every way into him who is the head, into Christ, from whom the whole body, joined and held together by every joint with which it is equipped, when each part is working properly, makes the body grow so that it builds itself up in love' (Eph. 4:13-16).

> 'that we may present everyone mature in Christ' (Col. 1:28).

What we find cute, funny, and acceptable for a one-year-old might not be cute, funny, and acceptable for a twenty-one-year-old. It might be cute to burp when you're one, but probably not so cute when you're twenty-one. It might be funny to make faces at the person in the car beside you when you're one, but definitely not funny when you're twenty-one. It might be acceptable to spit out food when you're one, but not at all acceptable when you're twenty-one.

'It's time for you boys to grow up!' So exclaimed my seventh-grade science teacher after he discovered that my friend and I had snuck three dissected fish out of the science room and hung them on a string over the main walkway of our middle school. It was time for us to grow up!

I keenly felt the need for growth into maturity when, on my wedding day, my new father-in-law spoke these parting words: 'You take care of her. She's your responsibility now.' Gulp.

Growth into maturity is one of the best analogies for describing the Christian life—both for individuals and for Christian communities. The Apostle Paul describes it in Ephesians as: 'we are to grow up in every way into him' (4:15). Grow up into what? Into 'mature manhood, to the measure of the stature of the fullness of Christ' (4:13). Notice how saturated such language is with *inChristness*! Growth is 'into him.' The goal is to grow up until we reach the 'stature…of Christ.'

This means that after a while it isn't funny when we do things that might have been acceptable for us when we were young in the faith. For example, Paul says that we shouldn't be tossed back and forth by various winds of doctrine. Someone who has matured in Christ ought to be able to recognize false doctrine, and avoid it. Growth also means that we should move away from disunity toward unity, and away from superficiality toward a deeper knowledge of Christ (4:13). Furthermore, we should grow in speaking truth in love to one another (4:15).

But growth requires cooperation. We can't make ourselves spiritually grow any more than I can make the tomato plant in my garden grow—only God can do that. But we can seek to cultivate healthy soul-soil, water appropriately, and remove hindrances to growth (weeds). As we live in conscious awareness of our union with Christ, when we remember how utterly dependent we are on Him, and when we increasingly incline our wills, our minds, and our hearts toward daily dependence upon Him, we can expect to spiritually grow. My junior high science teacher was right; it was time for me to grow up. But he probably assumed I simply needed to try hard to be mature. The truth is that we'll only make spiritual progress as we acknowledge our dependence upon Christ, and live like we actually need Him to order and direct our ways, which we do. All growth into spiritual maturity is *in Christ*.

CHAPTER 56

LEARNING CHRIST

> 'But that is not the way you learned Christ!—assuming that you have heard about him and were taught in him, as the truth is in Jesus' (Eph. 4:20-21).

When did you first start learning about Christ? Did you grow up with parents who taught you about Jesus? Or did you start learning what the Bible has to say about Christ when you were a teenager? Or were you, perhaps, already an adult when you first began to learn about Jesus?

But, timing aside, when did you actually *learn Christ*?

Is there a difference between learning *about* Christ and *learning Christ*?

Yes, indeed. That difference may be represented in Ephesians 4:20-21. Paul's statement that his readers 'learned Christ' is unusual; I have never come across a sentence in ancient Greek literature that combines the word 'learn' with a person as its object (though I happily admit that I may have missed something!). It is possible, of course, to learn a fact, a theory, or various pieces of information. And you can learn *about* a person. But learn a *person*? This is what makes Paul's accusation so arresting: 'But that is not the way you learned Christ!' What does it mean to learn Christ?

Think about the verses that surround this expression. Paul's words about learning Christ immediately follow his reminder that Christians should not *walk* (his word) the way people in the world do—in futility and darkness and ignorance and hardness of heart (4:17-19). Suddenly he exclaims: 'But that is not the way you learned Christ!' Then he follows his outburst by reminding them that they had heard Christ, been taught in Him, and that truth is in Jesus (4:21).

Considering what comes before and after, we have to conclude that to 'learn Christ' involves both learning about Him *and* experientially knowing Him in daily life. Paul's words about *hearing*, being *taught*, and knowing the *truth* indicate the gospel message they had learned—that is, what they had learned *about* Christ. But his words about being taught *in Christ* and being careful about how Christians should walk suggest that learning Christ is also relational and practical. This means that learning Christ is both learning the truths about Christ and being relationally connected to Christ.

So when did you learn Christ? Like many people, you may have learned some content about Christ before you came into personal commitment to Christ. But if you're anything like me, you are still *learning Christ.*

Let's finish these reflections about learning Christ by allowing Paul's challenge to sink into our heads, hearts, and hands. If in fact we have *learned Christ,* we need to commit ourselves to stop living the way people in the world live and start living according to what we have learned. If we judge that our learning of Christ is lacking, we can recommit to learning all we can about Christ and reconnecting with Him relationally. If you're unsure how to do this, I encourage you to commit yourself again to spending time talking with Him about it (prayer) and reading the most-precious-of-all books which He has sent to help you build your relationship with Him (Scripture). Also, don't forget to spend time around others who have a deep and solid relationship with Christ. Accordingly, you and I will be reminded of what we have learned and the relationship into which we have entered. We will grow in conviction that we are intrinsically and relationally connected to Christ.

But we can only truly *learn Christ* if we deeply own the truth that we are united to Christ. That is, coming to learn Christ is based upon the fact that we are already *in Christ.*

CHAPTER 57

THE NAME OF JESUS

'giving thanks always and for everything to God the Father in the name of our Lord Jesus Christ' (Eph. 5:20).

'do everything in the name of the Lord Jesus, giving thanks to God the Father through him' (Col. 3:17).

'so that the name of our Lord Jesus may be glorified in you, and you in him, according to the grace of our God and the Lord Jesus Christ' (2 Thess. 1:12).

I was listening to the enthusiastic voice of my ten-year-old daughter, Grace. She had left a voice message for me—letting me know that there was something exciting she needed to tell me. 'Please call me back as soon as you can, Daddy.' Then, 'Well, I've gotta go. In Jesus's name, amen.' She suddenly realized her mistake and started laughing hysterically. I listened to her laugh for about a minute—and couldn't help laugh along as I listened to her hooting. I learned later that she had fallen on the floor because she was laughing so hard.

'In Jesus's name, amen.' We think so little about what this phrase means that it's easy to assume that it means nothing. Sometimes we use it simply as a formula to close our prayers, kind of like saying goodbye to God. But it's much more than that!

Jesus taught His disciples to pray to the Father in His name (John 14:13-14; 15:16; 16:23-26). I'm sure that Paul knew about praying in Jesus's name because he had learned about what Jesus Himself had taught. But the name of Jesus in the Bible doesn't only get applied to prayer, even if prayer is one of its most important applications (Eph. 5:20; 1 Cor. 1:2). The early disciples cast out demons in the name of

Jesus (Luke 10:17; Acts 16:18), and healed in His name (Acts 3:6; 4:10). Paul's early preaching gets described as being done 'in the name of Jesus' (Acts 9:27-28). For Paul, everything was supposed to be done 'in the name of Jesus' (Col. 3:17) with the aim that Jesus's name might receive glory among His people (2 Thess. 1:12).

But what does it mean to pray—or to do anything else, for that matter—in the name of Jesus? It means that we exercise the authority that was granted us by virtue of our union with Christ. It isn't power we already possess; the authority comes from being in Christ.

What's the difference between power and authority? A police officer doesn't possess the physical power to stop a moving car. But when he dons a uniform and raises his hand, he has the authority to stop an oncoming car. It's not because of his strength, but because he possesses a derived authority. A police officer's authority is only vested as it has been granted to him. He has authority—as we have authority—because it has been given to us by Another.

When we face warfare from evil spirits and exercise our authority over them in the name of Jesus, we do so as people in Christ. When we share the good news, our message reverberates in the listener because we proclaim God's message as people united to Christ. When we pray 'in Jesus's name,' we acknowledge that there is no way we can make the matters occur for which we pray. If God doesn't answer our prayers, our requests won't be granted. But the Father gladly hears and answers the prayers of His children because we are *in Christ*. In our union with Christ, we have been given authority to pray in the name of Jesus for things that are in accordance with God's will, and we can expect that God will answer such prayers.

Do you know, dear child of God, the authority granted you in the name of Jesus? That authority is yours because you are *in Christ*.

CHAPTER 58

HUMILITY IN CHRIST

> 'Have this mind among yourselves, which is yours in Christ Jesus, who... emptied himself, by taking the form of a servant... he humbled himself by becoming obedient to the point of death, even death on a cross' (Phil 2:5-8).

Two times in my life God has confronted me about pride. I don't mean that I've only been lacking in humility twice in my life. Heavens no! But twice in my life God has made it a point to expose hidden pride and remind me of the example of Jesus, who left heaven and took the greatest step in the direction of humility ever taken in history—God becoming human. Let me tell you about the first time God exposed the reality of hidden pride in my life.

I was a young man living in a foreign country, trying desperately to learn a new language. My language-learning pattern included a couple of hours at home with a language helper, memorizing a few new sentences in the target language, then heading out on a language loop (shop to shop) to try to speak the sentences I had learned from my language helper.

The first day I said, 'Hello. My name is Ken. I am learning your language. This is all I can say. Goodbye.' I spoke these words in at least *forty* shops.

The second day I had a few more sentences to say: 'Hello. My name is Ken. I'm an American. I am learning your language. I spend my days in shops trying to speak. Can you help me? This is all I can say. Goodbye.'

Many times someone in the shop tried to talk back, but at least in the beginning, I hadn't yet acquired enough language to even provide a response.

Within a week, I could peer down a street and observe people starting to gather in shops I had previously entered —waiting for my arrival! I walked into shops already full of people silently waiting for me and trying oh-so-hard not to laugh. After reciting my lines and exiting, I couldn't even count to five before the shop exploded with laughter. Now *that* was humbling.

In the midst of this daily humiliation, I began to think about what Jesus said about the importance of becoming like a child (Mark 10:15; Luke 18:17). One thing is certain: my self-reliance, my sense that I was reasonably intelligent, and even my belief that I was an adult went out the window. God used this series of humbling encounters to remind me that Christ humbled Himself beyond anything I could imagine, and that I needed to pursue humility as someone connected to Him.

The Apostle Paul writes, 'Have this mind among yourselves, which is yours in Christ Jesus' (Phil. 2:5). If Jesus, who was 'in the form of God'—who had 'equality with God' (Phil. 2:6)—humbled Himself and became human, who am I to deem myself as worthy of special honor, or any honor at all? Note that some of our translations (e.g., ESV, NAB) go further by suggesting that we should take Paul's instruction to mean not merely that we should look to Jesus as our example, but that we should pursue humility on account of the fact that we are already united with Christ ('which is yours in Christ Jesus,' ESV). In other words, because we were united to Him, and thus share the humility of His crucifixion (like Gal. 2:20; Rom. 6:2-6), we need to pursue practical humility as people who are *in Christ.*

Oh, the depths of our pride! Even when we try to conquer our pride by being humble, we start congratulating ourselves for our newly discovered humility—and there it is again—more pride! But let us remember the example of Jesus and pursue humility *in Christ.*

CHAPTER 59

REJOICING IN CHRIST

> 'Finally, my brothers, rejoice in the Lord. To write the same things to you is no trouble to me and is safe for you' (Phil. 3:1).
>
> 'Rejoice in the Lord always; again I will say, rejoice' (Phil. 4:4).
>
> 'I rejoiced in the Lord greatly that now at length you have revived your concern for me' (Phil. 4:10).

'What are the joy-stealers? Why do so many of us struggle with joy?' I often ask my students this question when we open the book of Philippians.

'Time pressures.' 'Financial pressures.' 'Unfulfilled expectations.' 'Hurts from the past.' These are common responses from my students. But Paul would point us toward two other foundational reasons for our lack of joy.

First, Paul would advise us that one of the reasons we struggle so much with joy is that we don't rejoice enough. The themes of joy and rejoicing intertwine throughout the book of Philippians in such a way that a reader of that letter must conclude that joy and rejoicing are intricately connected to one another. We shouldn't think of joy as one thing and rejoicing as a totally different thing. Joy is the noun, and rejoicing the verb, but the basic idea is the same. Thus, if we want more joy in our lives, we should learn to rejoice more. But acknowledging that we don't rejoice enough is only the second-most-important thing we need to understand about our struggle with joy.

Paul would say that the most important reason we struggle with joy is that for most of us, our concept of joy is not 'in the Lord,' despite the fact that Paul keeps connecting his comments about joy to *in Christ*ness (3:1; 4:4; 4:10). Most of us strive for feelings of happiness, not in-Christ joy. Paul, you may remember, never tells us to 'just try to be happy.' Paul's joy is fundamentally linked to his union with Christ. He knows deep, lasting, and profound joy because he is *in Christ.*

If what I've written is accurate, this means that our joy in Christ is *not* dependent upon our circumstances. Paul is probably writing his letter to the Philippians while chained to a Roman guard under house arrest in Rome. He has been deprived of freedom for the previous three to five years (first in prison in Caesarea, then on a prisoner-transport ship, and now confined to a rented room in Rome). He has few external reasons to be happy. But he knows that he is *in Christ,* and so he repeatedly and insistently rejoices *in the Lord.*

Remarkably, even though joy in Christ cannot be diminished by circumstances, it can be increased. Paul indicates that his joy increases through friendships with others in Christ. Joy increases whenever he contemplates his warm, relational in-Christ connection to the Philippians (1:3-8; 1:25; 4:1). Joy increases whenever he learns that the gospel is spreading (1:18). Joy increases when he contemplates Christians living in unity (2:2). Joy increases when he discovers that the Philippians have decided to send him financial assistance during his incarceration (4:10-18). Joy even increases when he reckons with the possibility that his own sufferings are helping his friends in Philippi grow in faith (2:17). In other words, for those of us who know that we are already *in Christ,* there is no reason that our joy needs to be shaken. Instead, we should be encouraged to know our present joy can increase.

Friend, do you want more joy in your life? Learn to rejoice more. And whatever you do, don't forget to hold on to the truth that persistent joy is yours *in Christ.*

CHAPTER 60

EVERYTHING AS LOSS TO GAIN CHRIST

> 'But whatever things were gain to me, those things I have counted as loss for the sake of Christ. More than that, I count all things to be loss in view of the surpassing value of knowing Christ Jesus my Lord, for whom I have suffered the loss of all things, and count them but rubbish so that I may gain Christ' (Phil. 3:7-8 NASB).

Paul counted everything as loss because of his *inChristness*. You can feel his intensity in Philippians 3:7-8; passion reverberates off the page. But quite unexpectedly, for just an instant Paul starts to sound like an accountant. He writes that whatever he used to view as a *credit*, he now views as a *debit* because of Christ.

Do you normally think of accountants as passionate people? Stereotypically (and sometimes unfairly), we brand accountants as analytical, intelligent, organized individuals who love numbers more than people. Passion doesn't figure into the stereotype.

But I know one way to make an accountant passionate…quickly. Demonstrate to him that every time he thought he was adding, he was actually subtracting. All the money he thought he had in his managed account is gone. His account *owes;* there is no *gain* whatsoever. I dare say that your accountant is passionate now; he's breathing hard, starting to sweat, and pulling clumps of hair out of his already balding forehead.

Paul writes that his entire résumé as a devout and pious Jew— circumcised the eighth day, keeping all the laws that Pharisees were supposed to keep, so zealous for the law that he was willing to persecute those who didn't agree with him, viewed as blameless in his law-keeping (Phil. 3:5-6)—he now counts all of it as loss because of his union with Christ.

But Paul intensifies the contrast. His losses are not only debits, they are *skubala*. That's the Greek word, and it sounds gross, doesn't it? This word normally refers either to the household garbage (like all the gross stuff leftover on your plate after a meal), or to what gets eliminated from your body a couple of hours after the meal has been eaten (excrement; dung). All the things Paul formerly counted as a credit, he now not only views as debits, he deems them worthy only of the refuse dump or toilet.

But wait! After our hypothetical accountant discovers that he has been pressing the subtract button every time he thought he was trying to add, he makes an amazing discovery. While scrambling to ascertain the true state of his accounts, he comes across one account that is so loaded and so valuable that all his losses become as nothing compared to the assets in that one account. What he gained through no effort of his own is of infinitely greater worth than all the other accounts he lost. His losses are nothing in comparison to what he gains.

Jesus would have said that our accountant has stumbled upon a treasure in a field (Matt. 13:44). He has discovered a pearl of great value (Matt. 13:45-46). Henceforth, he can only view his résumé, possessions, and valuables as less-than-worthless, because the treasure he has gained is Christ Himself.

Oh, Christian brother or sister! Are you clinging to the illusion that your résumé is of any comparison to the life you have gained in Christ? Have you discovered that your own value is based solely upon the only One who deems your life worthwhile? Everything else is of such lesser value than Christ—no, it is of no value whatsoever by comparison.

Knowing that Christ is more valuable than everything can fuel your passion to know Him more and to live always and only for Him. Count everything else as loss because you are *in Christ*.

CHAPTER 61

KNOWING CHRIST

> 'the surpassing worth of knowing Christ Jesus my Lord' (Phil. 3:8).
>
> 'that I may know him' (Phil. 3:10).
>
> 'that the God of our Lord Jesus Christ, the Father of glory, may give you the Spirit of wisdom and of revelation in the knowledge of him' (Eph. 1:17).

The surpassing worth of knowing Christ Jesus my Lord. I love this expression! It is one of my favorite phrases in all of Scripture (Phil 3:8). What is more valuable than knowing Christ Jesus? Is there anything in the universe that rivals knowing Christ?

When my children were young, I used comparatives to help them grasp how much I cared for them and wanted a relationship with them. 'Do I love you more than my computer?' 'Yes!' they replied, 'You love us more than your computer!' 'Do I love you more than my guitar?' 'Yes! More than your guitar!' 'Do I love you more than my car?' 'Yes! You love us more than your car!' (That one was easy, it was an old Mazda minivan…) 'Do I love you more than all my books?' 'Yes, even your books!' To drive home my message, I sometimes added: 'I love you more than everything in the world!' My daughters, of course, wanted to make sure I was telling the truth, so they would probe: 'Except Jesus?...and Mommy?' 'Yes,' I replied, 'more than anything in the world except Jesus…and Mommy.' I wonder if we need to reclaim this sort of exuberance when we describe the incredible privilege of knowing Christ.

Listen to a few translations of Paul's superlative: *the excellency…the far greater value…the surpassing worth…the infinite value.* How can words communicate the incomparable privilege of knowing Christ?

The knowledge talked about here is not head knowledge. Otherwise, why would Paul refer to Jesus as *my* Lord? This expression is surprisingly personal, especially when one considers that Paul is speaking about his Lord and master—dare we say?—his owner. But that very master invited him, and us, into personal friendship. Our Lord Jesus doesn't want us to serve Him at a distance. He has summoned us into His presence and wants us to know Him personally. It's astounding, if you stop and think about it. He isn't too busy. He doesn't have better things to do. He wants a knowing relationship with Him. I want that too… so much! Don't you?

I remember a time in college when a certain professor—a very busy man who had the respect of all my peers, and with whom I desperately wanted to spend personal time—invited me to meet with him once a week for a year. He invited me to know him! Oh, how I looked forward to those meetings every week. Nevertheless, the access that godly man gave me into his personal space is nothing compared to the privilege of knowing Jesus.

The surpassing worth. The incredible privilege. The infinite value. What can possibly compare with knowing Christ?

Is knowing Jesus more valuable to you than everything in the world? Is the privilege of growing in your knowledge of Christ more precious to you than your guitar or your car (even assuming that you own a guitar and that your car is better than mine was)? Is friendship with Jesus worth more to you than your gadgets, your career path, your relationships? Do you value knowing Him enough that you take time to open up your heart to Him in prayer, eagerly listen to His Word, and keep seeking an awareness of His presence during your day? Is knowing Jesus better than everything else?

It is. And more. Jesus has invited us to know Him. The greatest value we will ever know in life is found *in Christ*.

CHAPTER 62

PEACE OF CHRIST

> 'And let the peace of Christ rule in your hearts, to which indeed you were called in one body' (Col. 3:15).
>
> 'And the peace of God, which surpasses all understanding, will guard your hearts and your minds in Christ Jesus' (Phil. 4:7).

'How are you today?' Like many of you, I hear this question many times a day.

The expected response to this question when I was growing up was, 'I'm fine, thank you.' Now, most of my students in California simply say, 'I'm good.' (Let the record show that I have never really appreciated this bit of slang; I hear Jesus's words ringing in my ears, 'No one is good except God alone.')

But sometimes when I'm asked, 'How are you?' I don't feel like replying with the standard 'I'm fine' or 'I'm good.' That's because I'm not always fine. (I'm certainly not always good!). This does not mean, however, that things at that moment are bad in my life, simply that... it's complicated.

I'm writing these words while waiting in an auto shop—an hour longer than promised—for a simple oil change. A talk-show host on the television in the corner is discussing in horrifying detail some recent assaults of a serial killer.

'How are you, Ken?'

Well, on the one hand, I'm unhappy that I have been sitting here for the past two hours. I feel the urge to get home to my wife who is concerned about and preparing for a medical procedure scheduled for tomorrow morning. I also wish that lightning would strike the power lines outside the car shop and send an electrical surge to fry the television set. At the same moment, I'm at peace in my soul, trusting in the Lord, open-hearted, and praying my way through this time of waiting—even as I write these few words to you.

Is it possible to be sad and happy at the same time? Can a Christian grieve and still hope? Can a follower of Jesus experience sorrow and peace together? Yes indeed. One of the great benefits of the *in-Christ* life is a foundational peace that undergirds and surrounds us even when our surface emotions are turbulent. Paul describes his own life as 'sorrowful, yet always rejoicing' (2 Cor. 6:10). In one of his letters, he expresses 'great sorrow and unceasing anguish' in his heart over the unbelief of his countrymen (Rom. 9:2-3), whereas elsewhere he instructs us to rejoice always (Phil. 4:4), and then a few verses later promises that when we bring our anxieties to the Lord in prayer that God's peace will guard our hearts and minds in Christ Jesus (Phil. 4:7).

But what about during times of profound loss, like grief over the death of a loved one who is a Christian? Yes, then too. Paul writes to those in Thessalonica who had suffered such a loss: 'that you may not grieve as others who have no hope' (1 Thess. 4:13). Please don't misunderstand. Christians still grieve, sometimes deeply. But our grief is different from those who are outside of Christ. We grieve *with hope*.

Solid peace is a real thing because it isn't dependent upon our presenting emotions. For those who truly know Christ, such peace is rooted in their *inChristness*. What God calls us to do, then, is to rest in the truth of our union with Christ, ask for the Holy Spirit to mediate that truth to us, and allow the peace of Christ to rule in our hearts, both individually and corporately (Col. 3:15).

Fortunately, the television host has now switched away from her piece about serial killing and has begun to discuss the recent public embarrassments of a popular social butterfly. Unfortunately, I'm still waiting for my car. But I am also thankful that I am undergirded and surrounded by the peace I have come to know *in Christ*.

CHAPTER 63

CONTENTMENT THROUGH CHRIST

> 'I can do all things through him who strengthens me' (Phil. 4:13).

It is one of the best-known verses in the Bible. It appears on wall art, bumper stickers, social media profiles, and even tattoos. But we usually misinterpret it.

Philippians 4:13 is not about personal empowerment. It is not a promise that you can become anything you want when you grow up if you want it badly enough. It certainly isn't assurance that you'll win an athletic contest or find success in your job. Quite the opposite is the case. In Philippians 4:13, the Apostle Paul models contentment in *whatever* circumstances he finds himself, whether things are going well or poorly. Moreover, the focus of this verse isn't on you or me… or Paul for that matter. The focus is on Christ who strengthens for contentment.

How do I know that contentment in any situation is the central issue in Philippians 4:13 rather than empowerment? Look at the verses that come just before (and pay attention to the words highlighted in italics): '…I have learned *in whatever situation* I am to be *content*. I know how to be *brought low*, and I know how to *abound*. In *any and every circumstance*, I have learned the secret of facing *plenty* and *hunger*, *abundance* and *need*' (Phil. 4:11-12).

It is only after Paul writes about contentment despite circumstances that he pens the words: 'I can do all things through him who strengthens me' (Phil. 4:13).

That Paul is writing about non-circumstantial contentment in this well-known verse is confirmed by the following verse: 'Yet it was kind of you to share my trouble' (Phil. 4:14). Paul thanks the Philippians for sharing his sufferings through financial aid. He is chained to a guard and needs external aid to provide food and clothing. Philippians 4:13, thus, cannot be about personal success; it must be about contentment despite one's circumstances, even if those circumstances include chains.

What Paul intends to say, then, is that through Christ he can be content despite his circumstances. No matter how hard it gets. No matter whether things are going swimmingly (as my English friends sometimes say) or are kinda' a drag (as we sometimes say in America). Paul is content. You can be, too—regardless of your circumstances.

But where does such contentment come from? This is a deeply personal question since many of us struggle with contentment. I know I sometimes do. When things are hard, I long for escape. When things are OK, I wish they were better. When things are good, I want them to be great; good isn't enough for me. Wretched man that I am! Who will deliver me from this discontent?

Thanks be to God through Jesus Christ our Lord! The only way…the *only* way…to break free from the incessant desire for better and more, from the constant longing for comfort and ease, is 'through him who strengthens me' (Phil. 4:13). What an astounding faith affirmation! As we depend upon Christ, whether our circumstances are easy or hard, Christ strengthens us to persist and persevere, to rest and rejoice, to be constant and content.

Precious brother or sister, is your life marked by contentment? Is rest and trust—whatever the circumstances—a defining characteristic of your life? Have you learned to be content regardless of the circumstances?

If you sense that God is calling you into a deeper life of contentment, let me encourage you to start leaning into the truth of your *inChristness*. You can only move toward profound contentment during the ups and downs of life when you focus on the truth that when you came to Christ you were united with Christ. You will discover strength from Christ to be content, despite your circumstances, as you deeply rest in the truth that no matter what happens, you are *in Christ*.

CHAPTER 64

NEEDS SUPPLIED IN CHRIST

> 'And my God will supply every need of yours according to his riches in glory in Christ Jesus' (Phil. 4:19).

Philippians 4:19 doesn't say that God will provide everything you *want*. It doesn't say that he will provide everything you *think* you need. It doesn't even say that God will provide all the alleged 'basic needs' that appear on Maslow's hierarchy of needs!

The verse says that 'God will supply every need of yours according to his riches in glory in Christ Jesus.' This means that everything that *God* knows you need will be provided according to His vast riches. But how do we gain access to those riches? The verse tells us it occurs 'in Christ Jesus.' You have access to God's riches because you are connected to Christ.

This means that there will never be a situation in which God does not provide for the needs of an in-Christ child. Even if you fail to receive what you *think* you need, even if you suffer or die along the way, you can be utterly confident that God knows what you truly need and has promised to provide.

During my first three years as a college professor, I started at the lowest faculty rank, with its correspondingly low salary. On my salary alone, my little family of four (at that time) could not hope to meet all our modest monetary needs in expensive New York, despite the fact that we knew how to live simply after years of overseas ministry and scraping through graduate and post-graduate school. We found ourselves living in New York in a situation where we definitely needed God to provide for our needs.

That's when the blessings started to flow. So many blessings, in fact, that Trudi started a 'blessings list' in the back of her journal to keep track of them all. On the side of the road, we found a reclining chair for our living room, a dresser for one of our daughters, and even a brand new pair of hiking boots that one of my girls was able to wear in the mud and snow for three years. Many needs were provided through the generosity of Christians: a used winter coat that I ended up wearing for longer than I want to tell you, a power mower for the lawn, bags full of used clothes for our daughters, and an anonymous check for $1,500 from 'friends' at the college who 'believed in what we were doing.' I noticed an $80 leaf blower tagged in a store for only *nine* dollars. After I drew the mistake to the attention of the manager, he sold it to me for nine dollars anyway! One of our struggles was to pay for birthday gifts for other children when our daughters went to birthday parties. But one day, an older faculty member dropped off at our house a box of fifty or so 'beanie babies' straight from the factory (tags and all!). From then on, our girls had appropriate gifts to give as gifts. (Don't worry, each daughter got to choose a couple of beanie babies for themselves!)

In all honesty, God did far more than simply provide for our needs during that lean period. He reminded us almost weekly that in Christ Jesus He was there to provide for us if we ever faced a true need. He taught us once again to trust that Christ is the One through whom all needs are supplied. We learned that we have access to the overflowing treasury of our glorious God because we are connected to Jesus. If ever we faced a true need—not a want, not a perceived need—God would possess ample provisions to meet that need. And how does He provide? He provides according to His riches in glory *in Christ*.

CHAPTER 65

WALKING IN CHRIST

'Therefore, as you received Christ Jesus the Lord, so walk in him' (Col. 2:6).

Walking is an important part of my life, despite the fact that I live in Southern California where it is difficult to get anywhere without a car. In truth, I enjoy walking. I walk to classes and meetings on the university campus where I teach. For eighteen years I walked to and from work, since I lived relatively short distances from the two universities where I have taught full-time. During my overseas years, my wife and I did not even own a car; every outing was via bus, shared-taxi, boat, train… or, most commonly, on foot. The most important walks in my life, however, have taken place in the early mornings when I walk for the purpose of prayer. Walking for prayer is good for me. It is, in fact, my favorite prayer-posture. It keeps me alert and focused. But after more than thirty years of such prayer-walking, I have found myself not only thinking about the importance of prayer, but also of the significance of Paul's metaphor of walking as an overall description of the Christian life.

You see, the Christian life is not a frantic rush to get to a meeting, nor, conversely, is it lounging by a pool at a resort. The pace of the normal Christian life can best be compared to a purposeful walk. Not a stroll—a walk. Not race-walking like you see once every four years during the Olympic Games. (Is that even a sport? Really? The only people who win that 'sport' are those who transition from walking to running at some point, which is, apparently, against the rules!) Granted, there are other metaphors to describe the Christian life—and there are times in our lives when we should run, and other times rest— but walking is one of Paul's favorite ways to describe *in-Christ* life. He even uses the Greek word for 'walk' thirty-two times.

But Paul doesn't want us to 'just do it,' as one sports company labeled the key to becoming a successful athlete. The way Paul puts it is quite different: 'Therefore, as you received Christ Jesus the Lord, so walk in him' (Col. 2:6). I sincerely hope that by this point in the book you have begun pausing whenever you encounter the words 'in Christ' or 'in him' while reading your Bible. This verse does not say, 'You've received Christ, now live it out.' Rather, what Paul actually writes is, 'As you've received Christ…so live your life *in him*.'

One way of envisioning this *in-Christ* connection is to imagine Jesus at your side when you walk through the regular activities of your day. It makes sense to imagine this, since Jesus is in fact with you by His Spirit!

So when you walk out the front door of your house, imagine Jesus walking next to you. When you enter the doorway of your school or workplace, He accompanies you. When you approach the front door of your church, He isn't waiting impatiently for you to come into His house; He walks with you to the door, opens it for you, strolls into church with you, and sits down next to you. When you exit a painful conversation in which someone unjustly attacks you, Jesus is with you; He was there when you received the attack, and He is right beside you as you walk away in anguish. When you saunter alone through a shopping mall (despite the crowds of people) in an attempt to ward off feelings of loneliness, you are not walking alone. Jesus is with you.

Receiving Christ Jesus was the most important thing you did in your entire life. The second most important thing you will ever do is learning how to walk *in Christ*.

CHAPTER 66

LIFE IS CHRIST

> 'Christ who is your life' (Col. 3:4).
>
> 'For to me to live is Christ' (Phil. 1:21).
>
> 'And whatever you do, in word or deed, do everything in the name of the Lord Jesus' (Col. 3:17).
>
> 'to remind you of my ways in Christ' (1 Cor. 4:17).

'What do you want out of life?' The trained interviewer appeared relaxed—even casual—as she asked me this question, but I could tell she was intent on figuring out who I was. In the context of interviewing for a summer job at a local department store during my break from college, that only meant that she wanted to ascertain my (then meager) work history, size up my personality and character, and decipher whether I had what it took to work in her department. The following day, she offered me a part-time job, but I turned it down when I got a better opportunity to work full-time at an electronics company. But the interviewer's question hung in the back of my mind.

I recently talked with a somewhat-older woman who had drawn up a 'bucket list' of what she wanted to do during her later years of life. I gathered from our conversation that her list included places she wanted to visit and fun activities she wanted to do. But nothing in our conversation suggested that Christ was at the center of her bucket list—or even anywhere *in* the bucket, for that matter. That conversation has been hanging in my mind recently.

What is life? Paul's response to that question is obvious in Colossians 3:4: 'When Christ appears—your life—then also you with him will appear in glory.' This is the literal order of the Greek sentence of the verse. Notice that Paul interrupts his thought about the return of Christ to accentuate the truth that *Christ is your life.*

When Paul contemplated the real possibility that his detention in Rome might end in death, he wrote: 'For to me to live is Christ and to die is gain' (Phil. 1:21). We often miss the important first bit of this verse because we get fixated on the second bit, the part about going to heaven after death. But we must not miss what comes before. Paul's first words are 'for to me'—indicating the personal nature of what comes next—followed by the words 'to live...Christ' or translated differently 'living...Christ.' Paul's sole reason for existence, he boldly declares, is Christ!

Such a Christ-focused existence is not esoteric; it impacts daily life. Paul off-handedly reminds the Corinthian believers of 'my ways in Christ' (1 Cor. 4:17). He encourages the Colossians to do *everything* in the name of the Lord Jesus—and makes sure they know that 'everything' includes their speech and actions: 'whether in word or deed' (Col. 3:17).

What do you want out of life? Now I'm repeating the question asked me during my department store interview. Or perhaps I should ask you, from my other conversation, what is on your bucket list?

How about a bucket list of one life-defining item? *I want to live my life entirely for Christ.* Put that on a piece of paper and drop it into your bucket! Better, get a permanent marker and write 'For to me to live is Christ' in bold letters on the outside of the bucket! Then, don't put anything into your bucket unless you know how it connects to your central life purpose of living life in, through, and for Christ.

Setting aside time to consider how other activities fit with your central life purpose will require prayer, reflection on the Word of God, and counsel from other Christ-centered Christians. But such time will be well-spent. Life *is* Christ and everything else is secondary for those who are *in Christ.*

CHAPTER 67

PHYSICALLY DYING IN CHRIST

> 'For if we believe that Jesus died and rose again, even so God will bring with Him those who have fallen asleep in Jesus' (1 Thess. 4:14 NASB).
>
> 'And the dead in Christ will rise first' (1 Thess 4:16).

What is the difference between dying in Christ and dying without Christ? Paul wrote some helpful words to the Thessalonians who had expressed concern about the fate of Christians who had died before the return of Christ. Paul assured those Thessalonians that anyone who had 'fallen asleep in Jesus' would be raised with Jesus. He added that anyone who had died 'in Christ' would rise again (1 Thess. 4:14, 16).[19] He wanted the Thessalonian Christians to know—and would want us to know as well—that those who are in Christ will surely be raised by Christ to future life with Christ.

One night when I was a young man, I dreamt a vivid dream. In the dream, I was a sailor working on a dock, such as I have always imagined at Pearl Harbor in Hawaii. Suddenly, planes filled the horizon and bombs began to explode all around me. I searched for a place to hide, but there was none. I was utterly exposed. An attacking plane banked and dove straight in my direction, firing as it approached. I knew in that moment I was going to die. I was certain that I was facing my final moment of life.

Now, there is a reason that this dream is still precious to me to this day, and why I have never forgotten it. That is because in the moment when I knew I was going to die, I also knew that I was ready to die. I was assured that if a bullet pierced my heart, or a bomb blew me into pieces, or I died under the crash of a kamikaze plane, my death would be *in Jesus* and I would one day be raised *with Jesus*. I knew in that moment that I would spend eternity with my Lord and Savior whom I had longed my whole life to see. Nothing as trivial as a bullet or bomb was going to hinder that. Death, the great enemy of humankind, could not stop it. I was in Christ, and I knew I was in Christ. I was not afraid to die.

What is the difference between dying in Christ and dying apart from Christ? The Bible teaches that the one who dies in Christ has no reason to fear death (Heb. 2:15). The one who dies in Christ can be assured that he will see his Christian brothers and sisters again—and considering the length of eternity, that day will be relatively soon! The one who dies in Christ can be comforted that her life is inseparably linked to the only One who can carry her through to a place of rest at the end of her sufferings. The one who dies in Christ can be certain that Jesus will be present throughout the entire ordeal of death, no matter how unsettling or lengthy or painful.

If you are *in Christ*—and I sincerely hope that you truly are in Christ—you have every reason to live in hope as you near the death that awaits everyone. This is because you were united to Christ before your death, you will still be joined with Christ as you near death, and you will forever be with Christ after death. Jesus, who has been with you throughout your life, will still be with you when you physically die. This is because, and only because, you are *in Christ.*

3

COMMUNITY
AND MISSION
IN CHRIST

CHAPTER 68

ONE BODY IN CHRIST

'so we, though many, are one body in Christ' (Rom. 12:5).

'Because there is one bread, we who are many are one body, for we all partake of the one bread' (1 Cor. 10:17).

'Now you are the body of Christ' (1 Cor. 12:27).

'And he is the head of the body, the church' (Col. 1:18).

'you were called in one body' (Col. 3:15).

A ship rescued a man marooned alone on a desert island for years. Before he set sail, the man wanted to show the crew around the island. When the captain noticed that there were three huts, he asked, 'What's the first hut for?'

'That's my house,' replied the man.

'What's the second hut for?' asked the captain.

'That's my church.'

'Then what's the third hut for?' asked the captain.

'Oh, that?' answered the man, 'That's the church I *used* to go to.'[20]

Now that we've shared an uncomfortable laugh, let's consider why this oft-repeated story is funny. It's funny because it feels *wrong*! Shouldn't we unite, not divide? Aren't we one body in Christ?

The Apostle Paul frequently refers to Christians as a 'body.' That is, *one* body, not two or three, or... 33,000, the number of Christian denominations listed in the World Christian Encyclopedia!

Since we've mentioned denominations, maybe we should inquire how to solve the problem of so many Christian groups. When asked about it, one fast-thinking professor quipped, 'You leave your church and join mine.' The reality is that resolving our differences is not as easy as joining hands and singing, 'We are one in the Spirit, we are one in the Lord.' Some differences are difficult to resolve. There are even differences that *ought* to divide us from other professing Christians. Knowing how actively to pursue practical unity often comes down to how important a potentially-divisive issue is. 'Did Jesus rise from the dead?' Yes indeed! On this, the Bible is emphatic and clear. You say no? OK, then I'm afraid we have no choice but to separate, at least in terms of *Christian* fellowship.

While we need to acknowledge that sometimes separation is necessary, the Bible still urges us to pursue tenaciously a practical unity rooted in our shared union with Christ. Let's not separate over small things, such as whether to serve coffee before church services or what color to paint the walls in the worship center. I admit that the hardest issues to negotiate are the mid-level difficulties of doctrine and church practice that must be decided church by church, such as modes of baptism or whether to allow public speaking in tongues.

The Bible calls us to exert *eagerness* in our quest to maintain unity (Eph. 4:3). Practical unity is based upon the inviolable truth that everyone who is in Christ is inextricably linked to every other true believer, no matter where that other believer lives, or what church he attends.

One thing I love about traveling internationally is that I regularly find myself surprised by how much unity we share in Christ. I once enjoyed an hour of fellowship with a Korean man on a ship in the Aegean Sea who couldn't speak English—and I don't speak Korean! Each of us communicated our unity in Christ by opening our Bibles and pointing to verses we each knew and loved. We even prayed for each other in our respective languages before bidding each other farewell. We sensed and shared spiritual oneness based exclusively on the reality of our shared union with Christ.

So let us pursue unity with each other—because we are in fact one body *in Christ*.

CHAPTER 69

CHURCHES IN CHRIST

> 'And I was still unknown in person to the churches of Judea that are in Christ' (Gal. 1:22).
>
> 'To the church of the Thessalonians in God the Father and the Lord Jesus Christ' (1 Thess. 1:1).
>
> 'For you, brothers, became imitators of the churches of God in Christ Jesus that are in Judea' (1 Thess. 2:14).

I teach at a Christian university. Some of my students think that since they receive Bible teaching Monday-Friday, they don't need to be involved in a local church on Sunday. Are they right?

What is a church? If you could ask Paul, his shorthand answer would probably be that a church is a gathering of people who are 'in Christ.' On that simplest of definitions, the Christian university where I teach is a church, since faculty, staff, and students profess to know Christ. Is that all there is to it?

Paul would reply, 'Yes and no.' Yes, according to Paul, the church is comprised of everyone who knows Christ, no matter where they live (Eph. 1:22; 5:25). This means that any time Christians gather they express the unity of the universal church. But don't forget that Paul expressly concentrates his attention in his letters on *groups* of Christians who gather together to worship, study God's Word, and celebrate the Lord's Supper. Such local churches are described by Paul as being 'in Christ.' For example, Paul writes about the (plural) 'churches of Judea that are in Christ' (Gal. 1:22; cf. 1 Thess. 2:14). Furthermore, Paul addresses the recently planted *group* of Christians in Thessalonica as those 'in God the Father and the Lord Jesus Christ' (1 Thess. 1:1).

So, although I may share a profound connection with any Christian who lives anywhere in the world because of our mutual *inChristness*,

I ought to connect and commit to a particular church in my locality. It's not much different from the way a father has more responsibility to care for the needs of his nearest relatives than for those of distant relatives, even if he loves and does what he can to care for them all.

Moreover, don't forget that the local church is essential for certain activities. This means that my Christian college students—and I, as a professor at a Christian university—still need to be active in a local church. For example, when I lead someone to Christ, where am I going to take them to grow? To the university? (Who's going to pay for their tuition?) What if I lose my way, allow sin to get a foothold in my life, and need someone to confront me—or even discipline me—and later restore me if I repent? With whom will I regularly share the Lord's Supper if not with members of a local church? How will I learn from Christians older and younger than myself—and permit them to point out blind spots endemic to my own generation—if I'm not involved in a local church? How will I make a long-term impact on foreign mission fields if I'm not linked together with other Christians who support the long-term work of God in the world?

My wife and I frequently relocated for education, work, and to fulfill God's calling on our lives during our earlier years of marriage. Every time we moved to a new city, our first order of business was to connect with a local church. Consequently, we have been closely connected to ten different local churches during our married lives. The church is universal, indeed, but it is also a local expression of God's rule over His people. We are not simply individuals swimming in a worldwide sea of believers; we are bands of Christians in every community who live out our *inChristness* together. We are churches *in Christ*.

CHAPTER 70

NO DISTINCTIONS IN CHRIST

'For there is no distinction between Jew and Greek; for the same Lord is Lord of all, bestowing his riches on all who call on him' (Rom. 10:12).

'There is neither Jew nor Greek, there is neither slave nor free, there is no male and female, for you are all one in Christ Jesus' (Gal. 3:28).

'Here there is not Greek and Jew, circumcised and uncircumcised, barbarian, Scythian, slave, free; but Christ is all, and in all' (Col. 3:11).

As I start this chapter I have just returned from a solemn assembly at the Christian university where I teach. This all-campus gathering was summoned by our university president so that our community might collectively lament the inequity, exclusion, isolation, and sometimes hostility felt by persons of color in our society, including at times on our Christian college campus. The instigation for this assembly was an extraordinarily insensitive decision made by someone a couple of weeks before to paint a swastika on the door of a dorm room shared by two students, one black and one white. As far as I know, the perpetrator never came forward, but the incident reminded us that people who are not members of a racial majority in whatever country they happen to reside often face marginalization and injustices, far more often than many people realize.

During the assembly, one perceptive student came to the microphone and offered a few poignant remarks about the climate of our university, a place she had evidently come to love deeply. This student reflected on how she came to realize that she was sometimes treated differently from other students because of her race. One of her comments was especially painful to hear: 'I knew I was a member of the body of Christ; I just felt like a different *kind* of member. Others were hands, and feet, and eyes; but I was different—like a scar.' It deeply grieves me that any Christian sister of mine would feel this way! Even though we are one body in Christ, some of our members are sometimes made to feel like they are only partial members.

But the Bible proclaims that there are no distinctions *in Christ*. We share the same standing before God. We are spiritual siblings. We all have the same Father.

Many of you who are reading this (though not all) will have been raised in a homogeneous culture, where the people you knew and associated with looked like you, talked like you, shared insider cultural knowledge, and experienced the privileges that inevitably attach to being an insider. What makes constructive dialogue about this topic difficult is that a person who has grown up as a member of a majority culture often doesn't know what it feels like to be in the minority. I have often commented to my wife that all of us should be required to live a portion of our lives as foreigners! It's only in such a setting that we come to realize that many things we assume are accessible to everyone are, in fact, not.

Since we cannot possibly expect everyone to live as a minority for an extended period of time, let me recommend that we make every effort to remind ourselves—over and over again—that *in Christ* we stand before God on equal ground as brothers and sisters, regardless of our ethnic or cultural heritage. We need to make intentional efforts to build relationships with people who are culturally different from us, despite the challenges that entering into such relationships will undoubtedly present. We are united together *in Christ*; we are brothers and sisters *in Christ*. There is no distinction in our standing before God, because we are *in Christ*.

CHAPTER 71

MINISTRY ROLES IN CHRIST

'For as in one body we have many members, and the members do not all have the same function, so we, though many, are one body in Christ, and individually members one of another' (Rom. 12:4-5).

'And he gave the apostles, the prophets, the evangelists, the shepherds and teachers, to equip the saints for the work of ministry, for building up the body of Christ' (Eph. 4:11-12).

'Tychicus the beloved brother and faithful minister in the Lord will tell you everything' (Eph. 6:21).

'And say to Archippus, "See that you fulfill the ministry that you have received in the Lord"' (Col. 4:17).

'I want to serve. I'm just not sure where.'

I was speaking with a young man who had recently moved to our city to study at the Christian university where I teach. He already understood the importance of the body of Christ and was starting to attend the local church where I worship and minister. Since I was an elder at the church at that time, he sought me out to discover ways he could get involved in ministry.

I guess I could have told him to find an online 'spiritual gifts test' and come back when he had 'discovered' what his 'gifts' were. But that actually wouldn't have helped since there is no biblical precedent for such a procedure. Paul never encourages people to try to 'discover' special abilities so they can start 'using' them in ministry. Abilities are not what Paul is writing about when he mentions 'gifts' anyway. Paul wants Christians to be aware that God has assigned every believer ministry-roles that will build up the body of Christ.

In the past few chapters, we have been reflecting on what it means to be one body in Christ. We have concentrated on our unity in Christ. In this chapter, I want to focus on the individual service roles each of us has been given on the basis of our *inChristness*. Every Christian has been assigned by God to differing ministry-roles that build up His church. The Apostle Paul doesn't focus upon the *abilities* to do such ministries, as many modern Christians tend to emphasize, but upon the *ministries themselves.*[21] I need you—and you need me—to strengthen the body of Christ by serving in our God-given ministries. Otherwise, the body doesn't function well.

Archippus was a member of the church in Colossae who may have stepped back from serving in his local house church. Paul wrote the same words to him as he would write to you or me in the same situation: 'See that you fulfill the ministry that you have received in the Lord' (Col. 4:17). God has at least one—and probably more than one—ministry-role for you. This doesn't mean that your ministries won't change over time. But it does mean that God has things for you to do. Get involved in ministry. Look for places where need, capacity, and desire come together—and then start serving. If you don't know which ministries are appropriate for you, talk to someone in leadership; a church leader can often help you find places where you can effectively serve.

The young man who approached me about serving in ministry started mentoring youth in our church. In that role, he was serving as a minister. The Bible views every believer in Christ as a minister; ministry is not just for pastors. Because of this, I can confidently declare that if you are not somehow serving in ministry—that is, over an extended period of time—you may be sidestepping, and thus violating, the biblical call to serve the body of Christ. God has good intentions for you, plans to use you to build His church. You can minister in the body of Christ—and have been called to do so—because you are *in Christ.*

CHAPTER 72

HOSPITALITY IN CHRIST

[concerning Phoebe] 'welcome her in the Lord in a way worthy of the saints, and help her in whatever she may need from you' (Rom. 16:2).

[concerning Epaphroditus] 'receive him in the Lord with all joy' (Phil. 2:29).

My wife is remarkably hospitable—far more than I. For ten straight years at her instigation, we invited *all* of my enrolled college students over *every week* during the academic year for dinner and spiritual conversation. (Fortunately, it never happened that they all showed up on the same evening. Whew!) We have scaled back a bit now, but still have lots of people, including my college students, over for dinners and other gatherings. Some of Trudi's hospitality stems from her love for people and her natural desire to be around others. I also think she absorbed the importance of hospitality during her years living in the Middle East where hospitality is a core societal value.

Hospitality is so highly esteemed in the Middle East that Trudi and I struggled for a while even to figure out how to share the gospel there. If you want to reach a neighbor in the United States, one of the best ways to get started is to invite your neighbor over to your house or apartment for tacos or barbequed steak. Such invitations are so unusual in American culture, especially in our cities, that neighbors are likely to think you're an unusually giving person, which sometimes opens the door to share Christ with them. But the hospitality of the average Middle Easterner exceeds the level of hospitality displayed by most American Christians, including ourselves.

The circles in which the Apostle Paul ministered, both Jewish and Gentile, highly valued hospitality much like contemporary Middle

Easterners do. But first-century Christians also added Christian love to their societally-conditioned impulse to be hospitable, often resulting in lavish and deeply sacrificial hospitality. It's no wonder that one of the requirements to serve as an overseer (elder, pastor) was that he be hospitable (1 Tim. 3:2; Titus 1:8).

Sometimes hospitality in the Bible focuses on care for outsiders, especially those in need (Heb. 13:2; James 1:27; Matt. 25:35-45). But the type of hospitality that intersects most closely with *inChristness* is Christian-to-Christian hospitality. It is a hospitality rooted in our shared connection to Christ. Thus, it is 'in the Lord' that we receive a brother like Epaphroditus (Phil. 2:29). Or when Phoebe comes to town, we welcome her 'in the Lord.' The great thing about Phoebe and others like her is that she herself is eager to show hospitality, so you may eventually become the recipient, not just the giver, of hospitality (Rom. 16:1-2).

Hospitality was so deeply valued by early Christians that if they could observe how many unhospitable people claim to be Christians in our generation, they would probably ask, 'Are you even Christians?' The idea that a Christian would *never* open his home, *never* share her food, and *never* bring people into the warmth and grace of *in-Christ* home life would be unthinkable to a first-century Christian.

Hospitality takes a lot of time, energy, and money…I know. Not only is my wife hospitable, now also are my daughters who picked up the value of hospitality from watching their mom. Literally thousands of people have passed through our home for student dinners, Bible studies, holiday celebrations, or just to 'hang out.' I'm eternally grateful that God sent me a hospitable wife to help me learn hospitality. Otherwise, I might have spent my life reading footnotes in old books in the basement of a university library.

In Romans 12:13, Paul reminds the church in Rome: 'Contribute to the needs of the saints and seek to show hospitality.' Paul's reminder—to them and to us—is grounded in the truth that we are *in Christ*.

CHAPTER 73

SPIRITUAL PARENTING IN CHRIST

> 'I do not write these things to make you ashamed, but to admonish you as my beloved children. For though you have countless guides in Christ, you do not have many fathers. For I became your father in Christ Jesus through the gospel' (1 Cor. 4:14-15).

> 'For children are not obligated to save up for their parents, but parents for their children. I will most gladly spend and be spent for your souls' (2 Cor. 12:14-15).

> 'my little children, for whom I am again in the anguish of childbirth until Christ is formed in you!' (Gal. 4:19).

> 'I appeal to you for my child, Onesimus, whose father I became in my imprisonment' (Philem. 10).

I have four daughters. Yes, four! I treasure my four daughters. I spend more time with them than with anyone else in the world except my wife. I sometimes rise early in the morning and stay up late at night for them. I expend money, energy, and countless prayers on my daughters. There are few things I wouldn't do for my four precious girls, even if the required sacrifice was great.

Not everyone reading this book has raised or will raise children. But all of us who name the name of Christ need to take seriously our roles as spiritual parents to those younger in the faith. Some people already do this extraordinarily well. An older woman in my church recently led a neighbor to Christ and has been spending large amounts of time with her new spiritual 'daughter'; they are reading and memorizing the Bible and praying through the challenges of new life in Christ. We need many more spiritual parents like her.

When the Apostle Paul wrote about spiritual parenting, sometimes he focused on the initial birthing of people into the spiritual family of God; that is, about bringing others to salvation. For example, he wrote that he became a spiritual father to the escaped slave Onesimus in prison by leading him to faith in Jesus Christ (Philem. 10). He also reminded the Corinthians that he became their father 'in Christ' because he introduced them to the gospel (1 Cor. 4:15). But Paul was determined not to act like a deadbeat dad who brought children into the world but later neglected to care for them. Instead, as a spiritual father he gave and guided, mediated and mentored, listened and led. Paul believed that spiritual parents were obligated to expend themselves for their children, and included himself in that commitment: 'I will most gladly spend and be spent for your souls' (2 Cor. 12:14-15).

Perhaps this would be a good time to pause and consider whether you are currently in any sort of relationship outside your own family in which you are spiritually fathering or mothering someone. Have you been bringing spiritual children into the world by introducing them to Christ? Are you spending time with those not as far along in the faith—feeding, supporting, and guiding? Can you name anyone to whom you are a spiritual parent right now?

You might be surprised to hear how many of my college students openly express a longing for spiritual parents, especially students who don't have parents who model vibrant Christian faith. Do you think you could become a substitute parent for a Christian college student? Or for the child next door who rarely sees or hears from his mostly-absent dad? Or for the middle school student in your church's youth group who currently is shutting out his parents and needs someone else to speak into his life? Take a moment and ask the Lord to show you whether there is someone near you whom you can help grow in the Lord. Let's reclaim—one person at a time—the ministry of spiritual parenting *in Christ*.

CHAPTER 74

SINNING AGAINST CHRIST

'Thus, sinning against your brothers and wounding their conscience when it is weak, you sin against Christ' (1 Cor. 8:12).

Did you know that when you commit a sin against a Christian sister you don't only sin against her? Were you aware that the Apostle Paul teaches that when you sin against a Christian brother you sin against Christ?

Where did Paul come up with an idea like this?

The idea didn't originate with Paul; he got the idea from Jesus. Jesus said that if you visit someone in prison, it's as though you visit Jesus. If you feed someone who is hungry, it is like you feed Jesus. If you help someone who is sick, it is like you care for Jesus (Matt. 25:34-40). Paul simply follows the logic of Jesus's words: if you sin against a brother or sister, it is like sinning against Christ.

Actually, it isn't just *like* it. Notice Jesus's precise words: '…as you did it to one of the least of these my brothers, you did it to me' (Matt. 25:40). Sacrificial service on behalf of others is not just *like* serving Jesus. Sinning against another Christian is not just *like* sinning against Jesus; it is, in fact, sinning against Him.

How can this be? It is because of our *inChristness*. It is based upon the fact of our union with Christ. Union with Christ is so fundamental to a Christian's identity—think only of the astounding truth that Jesus Christ actually dwells in every Christian through His Spirit—that a sin against someone who is connected to Christ is in fact a sin against Christ. What we do to another brother or sister, we do to Christ.

Paul wrote this warning in the context of first-century Christians trying to determine whether or not it was OK to eat meat that had first been sacrificed to idols. Suppose that a new Christian—a former idol worshipper—saw a longer-term believer eating meat that had been used as a sacrifice to an idol before it made its way to the meat market, and as a result the 'weaker' believer became emboldened to eat such meat himself even though he felt in his conscience that doing so might be wrong. When you influence a brother through your example to eat such meat—while his conscience is weak, writes Paul—you have sinned against Christ. It doesn't matter that it's just *meat* after all, even though that's true. Nor in such cases does it matter that food, including meat, is part of God's good creation, even though that also is true. If your brother has a weak conscience and you violate it, it's not just your brother against whom you sin; your sin is against Christ.

But what about freedom in Christ? Isn't this legalism?

No, legalism is something else. This is Christian love. You can still be confident that you have freedom regarding the so-called 'gray areas' (that is, the activities that the Bible does not specifically condone or forbid). But God has instructed you to be willing to limit your freedom out of love for a sister or brother. Paul was actually pretty radical about his willingness to limit his own freedom. He said, 'Therefore, if food makes my brother stumble, I will never eat meat, lest I make my brother stumble' (1 Cor. 8:13).

Suppose that Christ Himself was physically a member of your community group. You wouldn't knowingly sin directly against Him, would you? So why would you ever want to sin against a brother or sister who has been indwelt by Christ and whose connection to Christ is the most important thing about him or her? We will be far less prone to sin against one another if we keep at the forefront of our minds that our brothers and sisters are, like us, *in Christ*.

CHAPTER 75

COMMUNION IN CHRIST

'The cup of blessing that we bless, is it not a participation in the blood of Christ? The bread that we break, is it not a participation in the body of Christ? Because there is one bread, we who are many are one body, for we all partake of the one bread' (1 Cor. 10:16).

'For I received from the Lord what I also delivered to you, that the Lord Jesus on the night when he was betrayed took bread, and when he had given thanks, he broke it, and said, "This is my body which is for you. Do this in remembrance of me." In the same way also he took the cup, after supper, saying, "This cup is the new covenant in my blood. Do this, as often as you drink it in remembrance of me"' (1 Cor. 11:23-25).

I remember as a pre-teenager sitting on a Californian beach one evening in the 1970s observing a group of long-haired teenagers—'Jesus People' —singing simple songs of praise around a fire while one of them strummed a guitar. As their time of worship drew to a close, someone suggested that they share the Lord's Supper. So they did, right then and there. If my memory serves me correctly, the 'bread' they broke was a stack of Saltine crackers, and the 'wine' they drank was Coca Cola, since they had no other 'elements' on hand. That experience got me thinking about what is and what is not important regarding the meal instituted by the Lord for His disciples.

Did you know that the reason many churches refer to the Lord's Supper as 'communion' is because the Greek word *koinonia* (usually translated as 'participation,' 'sharing,' or 'communion') appears in 1 Corinthians 10:16, a passage where the Lord's Supper is mentioned? 'The cup of blessing that we bless, is it not a *koinonia* in the blood of Christ? The bread that we break, is it not a *koinonia* in the body of Christ?'

Participation in the Lord's Supper is sacred. It is not because bread and wine somehow magically turn into the actual body and blood of Jesus, as assumed by some Christians in history. Nevertheless, almost nowhere in our Christian experience does union with Christ get highlighted quite as clearly as it does through the symbolic act of communion. Some Christians believe that Christ is spiritually present in communion in a special way that He isn't at other times. But even among Christians who understand the act only to be a symbolic memorial of Christ's death and resurrection, it appears that they instinctively sense that the act in which they participate points to a deeper spiritual reality than simply remembering. For a short time, they are ushered into a moment of clarification that their union with Christ is of central importance to everything they do and are.

The next time you take the Lord's Supper, remember that this act gets to the heart of what *inChristness* is all about. It reminds forgetful people of the astounding truth that the benefits of the death of Christ include spiritual connectedness with Christ and, thereby, spiritual connectedness with other believers through Christ. Allow yourself to be amazed at, humbled by, and thankful for what Christ accomplished through His death on your behalf.

Even though I'm a lot older now, I still don't know whether Coca Cola and Saltine crackers carry enough symbolic weight to communicate the astounding reality of our union with Christ rooted in His substitutionary death. But I do know that the essence of communion is not in the morsel we chew or the liquid we drink. The Lord's Supper is a holy reminder—given to us by the Lord Himself—that the union we possess with Christ, and with each other through Christ, is a communion granted to us *in Christ*.

CHAPTER 76

CHURCH DISCIPLINE IN CHRIST

'When you are assembled in the name of the Lord Jesus and my spirit is present, with the power of our Lord Jesus, you are to deliver this man to Satan for the destruction of the flesh, so that his spirit may be saved in the day of the Lord' (1 Cor. 5:4-5).

The man had to be put under church discipline. He was, after all, sleeping with his father's wife! Worse, he was public and arrogant about it, but still wanted to call himself a Christian. She probably wasn't his mother, more likely his stepmother, and since men in those days often married younger women, the two may have been close in age. But this sexual liaison would have been abhorrent in first-century society. Jews would have been repulsed by it, aware that such relations were banned in Leviticus 18:8. Even upper-class Romans in the first century, whom we (rightfully) view as frequently condoning various forms of sexual immorality, considered such relationships off-limits. Cicero commented on a similar instance, the marriage of a woman to her son-in-law, 'Oh, the incredible wickedness of the woman, and, with the exception of this one single instance, unheard of since the world began!'[22] So when Paul commented that the sin of a man sleeping with his father's wife was 'of a kind that is not tolerated even among pagans' (1 Cor. 5:1), he wasn't exaggerating.

Something had to be done about it, so Paul challenged the Corinthian Christians to start the process of church discipline. Now, it's important to remember that church leaders don't simply decide to institute church discipline; they are to do it 'in the name of the Lord Jesus…with the power of our Lord Jesus' (1 Cor. 5:4). That is, their actions should come from their connection to Christ, since they are *in Christ*. In the well-known instructions Jesus gave about stages of church discipline (Matt. 18:15-20), the verb tense of Matthew 18:18 implies that church leaders are to get in line with what God has already determined rather than simply decide what to do: 'whatever you bind on earth shall [already] have been bound in heaven, and whatever you loose on earth shall [already] have been loosed in heaven' (*a literal translation with 'already' added for clarity*). The authority of church leaders to institute church discipline is derived from their *inChristness*.

Paul continues in 1 Corinthians 5 by adding these ominous-sounding instructions: 'you are to deliver this man to Satan for the destruction of the flesh, so that his spirit may be saved in the day of the Lord' (1 Cor. 5:5). Different interpretations of this verse have arisen because of various possible meanings of the word translated 'flesh.' Some interpreters understand 'flesh' to refer to a person's *body*. Paul would then be saying that the sinning man would be inflicted with some sort of physical illness or physically die. But many early church authors understood 'flesh' figuratively, especially since Paul often used the word non-literally to refer to a person's *tendency* or *desire* to sin. Also, there are hints in the passage itself that 'deliver this man over to Satan' means that they should separate him from explicitly Christian activities, such as from the Lord's Supper, group Bible reading, or shared times of prayer (note 'removed' [1 Cor. 5:2] and 'remove' [5:13]). Taken together, Paul is probably saying that if the man stops receiving the benefits of the Christian community, he might begin to feel the weight of living under Satan's influence and hit rock bottom, which will hopefully take away ('destroy') his desire to sin ('flesh'), so that he might repent and return to Christian fellowship.

Such church discipline is to be carried out by church leaders, supported by the congregation, who together are committed to maintaining the holiness of the church because they are *in Christ*.

CHAPTER 77

LOVING OTHERS IN CHRIST

> 'And walk in love, as Christ loved us and gave himself up for us, a fragrant offering and sacrifice to God' (Eph. 5:2).
>
> 'My love be with you all in Christ Jesus' (1 Cor. 16:24).

When I was a young man, my view of *really spiritual people* included such traits as radical discipleship, simple monetary lifestyle, passionate prayer, and bold witness for Christ. I still think all of these are important. But I was conspicuously missing some of the necessary ingredients in a truly spiritual life…like…um…*love*. In truth, the only reason I started to value love as vital to the Christian life was because I also believed reading the Bible was important, and I couldn't get around the fact that the Bible talks *a lot* about loving others. Gradually, through the conviction of God's Spirit working on my heart through the Word, I started to emphasize love more than I had in the past. That's a good thing, since loving others is basic to an *in-Christ* life.

But what is love—that is, Christian love? The first part of the biblical answer is straightforward: love *is* what love *does.* It isn't primarily a feeling; love is inextricably linked with loving actions. Love patiently bears with those who frustrate you. Love extends kindness. Love rejoices when others are successful and turns its heart away from envy and jealousy when others succeed. Love never insists on getting its own way. Love refuses to allow irritability and resentment to break apart a relationship. Love never gives up on someone. (See 1 Cor. 13:4-8 for these and more examples of love in action.) Love is what love does.

In Ephesians, Paul moves us a step further in understanding the nature of love. Paul says that we learn what love is by looking at the example of Christ. We 'walk in love, as Christ loved us and gave himself up for us' (Eph. 5:2). The love of Jesus was exhibited most astonishingly in the sacrifice of Himself—a sacrifice to death—for sinners like you and me. No wonder Charles Wesley, almost three centuries ago, responded to such thoughts with: 'Amazing love, how can it be? That thou, my God, shouldst die for me!'

Pause for a moment and consider the extent of that love! It is a love like no other. But let's take our meditation on love yet one further step. Not only do we learn that love is embodied in actions, and not only do we recognize that the extent of love was modeled by Christ, but we discover that in some incomprehensible way, the sacrifice of God's Son also *connects* us to Christ, which provides the means by which we can love others truly. That is why the Apostle Paul not only closed his first letter to the Corinthians with the words: 'My love be with you all,' but with: 'My love be with you all *in Christ Jesus*' (1 Cor. 16:24). He can extend love because he is—as are the Corinthians...and us!—united to Christ.

Take a moment and honestly ask yourself whether love characterizes your life. Suppose someone were to ask your sister to describe you. Would she style you as someone who loves others well? If a brother were asked to list the ten most loving people he knew, would you be on his list?

Honestly, I'm not sure I'd make such a list. Granted, I have grown in loving others. But I am painfully aware of how much I still need to grow in this area. I am personally acquainted with many Christians who love better than I do. I want to be like them, and to love like Christ loves. May you, dear brother or sister, grow in learning how to love others as an overflow of your in-Christ life. May you love others because you are *in Christ*.

CHAPTER 78

FORGIVING OTHERS IN CHRIST

'Indeed, what I have forgiven, if I have forgiven anything, has been for your sake in the presence of Christ' (2 Cor. 2:10).

'Be kind to one another, tenderhearted, forgiving one another, as God in Christ forgave you' (Eph. 4:32).

'if one has a complaint against another, forgiving each other; as the Lord has forgiven you, so you also must forgive' (Col. 3:13).

It wasn't a crime committed against me. It wasn't hateful or abusive or even anything that would probably shock you. But as days became weeks, and weeks became months, a Christian brother's deprecating words began to worm their way into my heart. I began to feel the fingers of unforgiveness reach toward my soul. Worst of all, I was fully aware it was happening. Still, I knew that unforgiveness toward a brother wasn't an option for me. I even knew that if I kept walking down the path toward unforgiveness it would lead to bitterness and the shrinking of my heart. Most of all, I knew that an unforgiving heart would dishonor God and tear at the seams of intimacy I shared with my Lord. But I was still struggling to forgive.

After unrelenting months of criticism and disparaging words, I seized upon an opportunity to spend a few months away from this individual. I determined to use those months to deal honestly and openly before God about my unforgiveness. Unfortunately, my naturally analytical disposition worked against me. You see, I *think* all the time, which includes mentally replaying past conversations and even sometimes making up hypothetical conversations that never actually transpired— and might never transpire. So in that state of mind, I was as likely to extend a once-for-all forgiveness from the heart as to swim successfully the English Channel. I came to understand that the only possible way I could forgive was 'in the presence of Christ' (2 Cor. 2:10).

So I committed the first portion of my morning prayer walks to forgive this particular brother *once again*. I found strength in Jesus's words that we should forgive 70x7 times (Matt. 18:21-22), which, for the non-math people reading this chapter, works out to 490 times! I should clarify that I understood that Jesus's words were hyperbole, and I also knew that the situation Jesus addressed wasn't even entirely parallel to my own, since this brother hadn't apologized. (I even knew that Jesus might have been using the number 77 instead of 70x7!) Nevertheless, I resolved to set out on a prayer walk each day to forgive this wrong 'one more time,' even if it required 490 days for forgiveness to settle in my heart. In truth it took two and a half months (around 75 days!) before a settled forgiveness took root. (I told you I have trouble letting things go...)

What was the most important thing that helped me forgive my brother? I recalled, again and again, the forgiveness I had received from Christ. I reminded myself that I needed to forgive *as Christ had forgiven me* (Eph. 4:32; Col. 3:13). My basis to forgive was my standing as one who had already been forgiven of all my sins through the sacrificial death of Jesus Christ on the cross. God used this incident to prepare me to respond many years later to someone who asked me to forgive him for a deeply egregious wrong: 'I most certainly forgive you. Jesus Christ has forgiven me so much; how could I withhold forgiveness from you?'

I'll be honest, it still isn't easy for me to forgive, but I've come to know the freedom that follows when I extend to others the forgiveness I have received from Christ. And so will you, if you remember that you can forgive any and all wrongs committed against you because you already stand forgiven *in Christ*.

CHAPTER 79

GENEROSITY THROUGH CHRIST

> 'For you know the grace of our Lord Jesus Christ, that though he was rich, yet for your sake he became poor, so that you by his poverty might become rich' (2 Cor. 8:9).

One ministry of the Apostle Paul that was close to his heart was his mission to collect relief funds for the poor and destitute Christians living in Jerusalem. This ministry of Paul is also one that many modern Christians know little about.

You will recall that Paul embarked on three missionary journeys to take the gospel to unreached peoples throughout the eastern Mediterranean. Those journeys get described in the book of Acts. But an important part of Paul's third missionary journey, although not mentioned directly in the book of Acts, was his program of collecting aid from the churches he had planted among the Gentiles in order to convey it to poverty-stricken Jewish Christians in Jerusalem. How do we know about this collection? We know about it from the three letters Paul penned during his third missionary journey (see 1 Cor. 16:1-4; Rom. 15:25-28; and most fully 2 Cor. 8–9).

You can tell from 2 Corinthians 8–9 that Paul planned to visit Corinth soon. In fact, it looks like he wrote 2 Corinthians while making his way toward Corinth, though he kept stopping to minister at other churches along the way. Paul and the Corinthian Christians already shared a long and rocky relationship leading up to the time he penned 2 Corinthians. Paul was the original church-planter of the church in Corinth (Acts 18). But in the intervening four or five years between planting the church and the visit envisioned in 2 Corinthians, he had been obliged to address, often from a distance, a host of problems in Corinth, such as internal divisions, Christian-against-Christian lawsuits, false teaching, and various kinds of immoral behavior. Now he is concerned that the church won't actually deliver upon a promise they had made one year previous to collect money for the harassed and impoverished Jewish Christians in Jerusalem.

So, in order to encourage the Corinthians to fulfill their pledge, Paul offered two powerful examples of sacrificial giving. The first was the example of Macedonian churches (like Philippi, Thessalonica, and Berea). Paul reported to the Corinthians that the Macedonians had financially sacrificed so they could give generously, despite many of them being terribly poor themselves. In fact, when Paul, on account of their poverty, tried to moderate their lavish giving, the Macedonians begged him to allow them to keep sharing in the ministry of giving (2 Cor. 8:1-5).

Paul's second example to help motivate the Corinthians was the example of Jesus. 'For you know the grace of our Lord Jesus Christ, that though he was rich, yet for your sake he became poor, so that you by his poverty might become rich' (2 Cor. 8:9). In the midst of encouraging the Corinthians to give generously, Paul pointed his readers to the extraordinary generosity of Jesus. This was not monetary generosity, but sacrificial-life generosity wherein Jesus 'became poor' so that spiritual riches might accrue to the Corinthians (and to us) by means of His sacrificial life and death.

In other words, our most important motivation as Christians to help us share with those in need is our connection to Jesus, who showed us what sacrificial giving looks like. Jesus made us spiritually rich 'by his poverty,' which is a picturesque and powerful way of describing the *inChristness* we have been meditating on for this entire book.

Why have so many Christians in history gladly shared their money and possessions with people in need? Christians share because Jesus sacrificed heaven for them. Christians share because Jesus provided a way for them to become spiritually rich. Christians share because they are *in Christ*.

CHAPTER 80

FAMILY IN CHRIST

'as a beloved brother—especially to me, but how much more to you, both in the flesh and in the Lord' (Philem. 16).

'Wives...as to the Lord' (Eph. 5:22).

'Husbands...as Christ loved the church' (Eph. 5:25).

'Children...in the Lord' (Eph. 6:1).

'Fathers...in the discipline and instruction of the Lord' (Eph. 6:4).

We Christians are so used to referring to each other as 'brothers and sisters' that we have forgotten how truly radical it was for early Christians to use this terminology.

In the first century, referring to someone outside your natural family as a brother or sister was countercultural. In an honor-and-shame culture where physical family was the central circle, your birth family was likely to get offended if you expressed familial loyalty to anyone outside the circle of your natural family. A really close friend could eventually get viewed like a brother or a sister; but addressing a random Christian you just met—who might be of a different social status than you—maybe even a slave!—as 'brother' or 'sister' would have been viewed as strange, and by some as undermining the social order. But that's what Paul did; he treated all believers in Christ as family members, and helped normalize this radical concept for Christians of all ages.

He learned it, of course, from Jesus who, when told that His mother and brothers were waiting outside to speak to Him, declared: 'Who are my mother and my brothers?' Then he looked around at those listening to His teaching and added: 'Here are my mother and my brothers! For whoever does the will of God, he is my brother and sister and mother'

(Mark 3:31-35). We should never underestimate the importance of viewing the church as the family of God.

I wrote these first paragraphs a day or two ago, and have just picked up the chapter in a hospital room. It is 6:00 a.m. and, mercifully, my wife is finally asleep. Trudi and I are on the back end of a sleepless night in a hospital emergency room because Trudi is experiencing a frightening allergic reaction to *something* the doctors do not recognize. She is not responding to medications, and her face, neck, and trunk are swelling with bright red painful rashes. Her eyes are almost swollen shut. We are waiting for a skin specialist who will hopefully be able to diagnose and recommend a course of action. We are nervous but prayerful.

But already we have received an outpouring of love and concern from the family of God. They really are our brothers and sisters. They care that Trudi is suffering. They are praying for her. Many have offered help. Some are on their way to the hospital as I write. We are thankful to be part of a family connected to one another through Christ! I often wonder how people who aren't part of this spiritual family negotiate the really difficult periods of life, like emergency visits to the hospital.

It is now a week since Trudi's emergency. The skin specialist arrived at the hospital shortly after I wrote those middle paragraphs. He tentatively diagnosed Trudi's condition as an extreme allergic reaction to *something* in the environment (to *what* is not yet clear), built upon a heat rash. Thankfully, after way-too-many medications, a week of rest, and many prayers from her family in Christ, she is doing much better.

Both of us have been reminded through this frightening event of how blessed we are to belong to a spiritual family. We have recommitted ourselves to living as full participants in our Christian family. We want to be there for our spiritual brothers and sisters when they face their own crises. We also want to be there as family when no crisis is on the horizon.

It is good to be members of a spiritual family constituted *in Christ*.

CHAPTER 81

AGREEMENT IN CHRIST

> 'I entreat Euodia and I entreat Syntyche to agree in the Lord' (Phil. 4:2).

They weren't getting along. They couldn't stop arguing with each other. At least that's the way it appears from what Paul wrote in Philippians 4:2: 'I entreat Euodia and I entreat Syntyche to agree in the Lord.'

The worst part about it was that at some point in the past these two women had labored alongside Paul in proclaiming the gospel (Phil. 4:3). But that was in the past; now they couldn't stop arguing. Euodia and Syntyche had become Odious and Stinky.[23] It had gotten so bad that Paul had to ask a member of the congregation to intervene to help resolve their dispute (Phil. 4:3).

What is it that Paul urged of these two women? He admonished them to 'agree in the Lord.' But what does it mean to agree in the Lord?

Does it mean that they have to share the same opinion about everything? Does it mean that they can't express disagreement when they think something isn't right? Not at all. All followers of Jesus Christ, of course, must share certain core convictions about the character of God, the person and work of Jesus, the way of salvation, etc. But it appears that these women already did agree on such things, otherwise Paul wouldn't be trying to get them back into gospel work.

Arguing among Christians is so common, that I can confidently assume that you know a couple of argumentative people who have become odious or stinky. I sincerely hope that the first person who came to mind wasn't *you*. Was it? Are you someone who frequently gets into arguments?

I recently heard someone comment about an older person: 'Oh him? Don't worry yourself about him. He's just contrary.'

How would you like those words said about you? Have they *already* been said about you? Worse, do you kinda' *like* getting into arguments? Are you sometimes Odious? Or Stinky?

Now, there is a difference between expressing necessary disagreement and arguing. The main difference often lies in the attitude in which a conversation takes place. A humble and gracious person can—and sometimes should—express disagreement when encountering something doctrinally or morally wrong, and even suggest an alternative path when a course of action appears unwise. But the primary attitudes of those who argue a lot are *pride* (wanting to win an argument) and *anger* (allowing frustrations from other areas of life to spill over into a conversation). So what should you do if you are regularly argumentative?

You can begin by confessing your pride and/or anger. But then what? Paul would answer that you need to learn how to agree 'in the Lord.' Stated differently, you need to remember your *inChristness*. Argumentativeness doesn't match the attitude of Christ who described Himself as 'gentle and lowly in heart' (Matt. 11:29). If you have been joined to Christ, you will increasingly want to take on the characteristics of the One to whom you are joined.

Furthermore, in the case of a discussion with another Christ-follower, remembering your *inChristness* will help you argue less since you'll be living in the awareness that both of you are connected to Christ, and through Christ to each other. You are brothers and sisters, members of the same family, all under a single head, Jesus. In practice, this means that you'll attempt to find common ground in whatever you are discussing, knowing that both of you stand before God on the common ground of Christ! As a consequence, you'll listen more carefully and seek to respond in ways that depict someone connected to Christ.

Do you want to be less argumentative? You'll argue less if you remember that you are joined to one another *in Christ*.

CHAPTER 82

AFFECTION OF CHRIST

'For God is my witness, how I yearn for you all with the affection of Christ Jesus' (Phil. 1:8).

Have you ever cared for a group of people so deeply that separation from that group almost hurts? That's the way I sometimes feel about living apart from my Christian brothers and sisters in the Middle East. Half my heart is in my teaching ministry in Southern California, while half of it is on the other side of the world. But I felt the same when I lived in the Middle East. Half my heart was there, and half was back home with my natural and Christian family.

Despite the relatively short time Paul spent in Philippi, it seems that he developed the same sort of affection for the Philippians as I feel for my Christian friends in the Middle East. His letter to the Philippians is exceptionally warm when compared to other New Testament letters. It is often described as a 'friendship letter.' Paul's letter overflows with affirmations of care for his friends in Philippi.

But a large part of the yearning to be with Christian brothers and sisters, both for Paul and for us, is not just that we have affection for someone we've come to know, but that we are relationally linked to someone else. In other words, it isn't simply affection in general, it is the 'affection of Christ Jesus.' We are linked to one another because we are individually linked to *Him*. *He* is the reason we have such affection for one another.

Have you ever attended a funeral of someone for whom you deeply cared and found yourself talking about your loss with a stranger who also knew the person you loved? You end up sitting at a table at the reception beside someone you've never met, and start asking each other how you were connected to the person who passed away. You share personal memories and receive encouragement from someone who only a half hour before was a total stranger—solely because each of you was joined in some sort of relationship with the person who had recently died.

Our fondness for one another as Christians is a little like that, and certainly more. What joins us together is our shared connection to Jesus. What links us is our *inChristness*. But unlike the person next to us at the funeral reception, our connection is through One who is alive and active and living in us by His Spirit. This means that whatever natural affection already exists is increased through our shared link to Jesus, since He by His Spirit places His affection in us. Johann Bengel stated it well: 'In Paul it is not Paul that lives, but Jesus Christ; wherefore Paul is moved not by Paul's but by Jesus Christ's affection' (trans. from Latin).[24]

And what an affection it is! My oldest daughter spent a year in the Southern Philippines (Mindanao) with openness to long-term work there. At her commissioning service, someone read over her Jesus's words, 'Truly, I say to you, there is no one who has left…brothers or sisters or mother or father or children…for my sake and for the gospel…who will not receive a hundredfold now…brothers and sisters and mothers and children' (Mark 10:29-30). Our connection to Christ means that others who know Him are family members—no matter where in the world we travel. My daughter received affection from brothers and sisters whom she had never formerly met, but who became her new family in an otherwise unfamiliar culture. How is it that such intensity of affection can be established so quickly? Such affection originates in our shared union *in Christ*.

CHAPTER 83

WORD OF CHRIST

> 'Let the word of Christ dwell in you richly, teaching and admonishing one another in all wisdom, singing psalms and hymns and spiritual songs, with thankfulness in your hearts to God' (Col. 3:16).

I sometimes wonder how different our churches might look if we actually did what we read about in the Bible. For example, when we gather together as believers in Christ, we are instructed to 'Let the word of Christ dwell in you richly' (Col. 3:16). Would obeying this verse impact the look and feel of our churches? Before we answer that, though, we need to address three questions: (1) What is 'the word of Christ'? (2) Is this a command to individuals or to the church as a whole? (3) How do the phrases about teaching and singing in Colossians 3:16 connect to the indwelling of the word of Christ? Let's briefly address each question and then address the question of how this verse might change the look of our churches.

First, the combination of 'word' + 'Christ' is uncommon in the New Testament, so 'the word of Christ' probably isn't a general reference to the Bible. It also probably isn't a reference to the words that Jesus taught during His earthly ministry, though that is grammatically possible. It is more likely that the word that gets communicated *is* Christ; that is, that Christ is the content of the word, like one translation renders the expression: 'the message about Christ' (NLT).

Second, the instruction seems primarily addressed to the whole congregation, as the words 'one another' in the following phrase make clear, but individuals are also in view since the command is to be carried out with thankfulness 'in your hearts' to God.

Third, the primary ways that the message about Christ can take hold and influence a local congregation (or in Paul's words, 'richly indwell' a congregation) is when everyone keeps teaching each other about Christ and keeps singing songs of thankfulness about Christ.

Back to our original question. Would our churches look different if we actually allowed the message about Christ to indwell the life of our churches? Oh, how different our churches would look! Imagine that most people in your church—not just the pastors or lay leaders—shared a personal mission to talk as much about Christ with each other as they possibly could. When they saw each other on Sunday mornings, they would direct their conversation toward Christ rather than toward sports or politics (or worse, gossip or backbiting). What if people were so excited to share what they were learning about Christ that they carved out time from their otherwise busy schedules just to talk to each other about Christ?

And what if—keep imagining with me—that we were so taken with the message about Christ that our congregational singing overflowed with genuine, from-the-heart thanksgiving for all that Christ has done for us? We could express heartfelt thanksgiving to God for the work of Christ and learn the great doctrines about Christ all at the same time. What a church that would be!

Beloved brothers and sisters, are you so taken with the message about Christ that you make time to get together with others who are of the same mind in order to teach and learn about the Jesus you claim to love so much? Are you searching out those not so inclined to talk about Christ in order to include them in the benefits of the message of Christ that is impacting your church? Are you so indwelt by the word of Christ that your singing overflows with thankfulness to God?

Oh, that we might allow the message about Christ to dwell richly in us in our teaching and our singing! May we increasingly experience this aspect of life *in Christ*!

CHAPTER 84

CHURCH LEADERSHIP IN CHRIST

> 'We ask you, brothers, to respect those who labor among you and are over you in the Lord and admonish you and to esteem them very highly in love because of their work' (1 Thess. 5:12-13).

Paul's appeal is gentle. He addresses the Thessalonians as siblings. He even asks them to do the thing he requests in an attitude of love.

But his request is difficult. At least for many of us who have a high opinion of our own opinions, this is a hard request. Paul requests the Thessalonians to show respect to those who are over them in the Lord.

Respect. Honor. Esteem. Not a critical attitude. Not undermining the church leaders' God-given authority. Rather, esteeming them for the work they do among us.

Notice that this request does not come *after* the leaders have first proven themselves to be respectable over a long period of time. Showing respect is a basic posture we should take toward whomever God has placed over us, because, according to 1 Thessalonians 5:12, our leaders are over us *in the Lord*. It's not about feeling respect, but about showing respect based upon our shared connection in Christ.

Trudi and I moved a lot during our younger years in response to God's call on our lives. As a result, we have been closely connected to ten different churches. One thing that has been a constant in each of these ten churches is that a few members in each church count it their right to criticize their church leaders as frequently and vocally as they want. Since I have served on leadership teams in a few of these churches, I have observed how much hurt has been generated by critical people. I have sat with pastors and their wives as they wept over unfair criticism they have received. I have personally been on the receiving end of some hurtful criticisms, though I know others who, far more than I, have been repeatedly and sometimes mercilessly maligned for doing nothing other than trying to lead their churches the best way they know.

If you sense a critical spirit in yourself, can I gently urge you to first talk to the Lord about it and ask Him to help you start down a new path of showing respect to your leaders? This does not mean that you cannot take legitimate concerns to your church leaders. You can, and in fact, you should. But please receive this as a gentle urging that you should remember that their labor among you is *in Christ,* and for that reason alone, you need to offer them respect *in Christ.*

Let me pause and briefly address any church leaders who happen to be reading this right now. Your *inChristness* is crucial to processing the criticisms of overly-critical people. When you remember that your position is *in Christ,* that your labor is *in Christ,* and that your service is *in Christ,* you can rest your heart *in Christ* rather than in the opinions of others. Yes, you should carefully attend to legitimate suggestions and corrections, but you do not have to bear unjust criticism alone. If you were indeed called by God to your place of leadership, then you were called *in Christ.* Remembering that you were called *in Christ* will help you through the hardest criticisms you might face.

I am afraid that critical people are not going away anytime soon. May you not be one of them. I pray that you will remember that the church leaders whom God has placed over you are serving *in Christ.* I pray that you will respond accordingly.

1 Thessalonians 5:12 is God's appeal to us: 'We ask you, brothers, to respect those who labor among you and are over you' *in Christ.*

CHAPTER 85

WELCOMING CHRIST

> 'and though my condition was a trial to you, you did not scorn or despise me, but received me as an angel of God, as Christ Jesus' (Gal. 4:14).

Two weeks after my wife and I married, we moved into a small apartment in the middle of an enormous four-block-by-two-block apartment complex in Portland, Oregon. This complex housed more than a thousand refugees from the wars in Southeast Asia. We located there to do ministry and to get some valuable training in cross-cultural communication before moving overseas.

Only a couple weeks after our move, Trudi was home alone when she answered a knock at the door. She opened to a policeman who wanted to ask her about a shooting that had taken place a month prior. 'You would have been able to see it clearly from your front window,' said the officer. 'Oh, I'm sorry,' replied Trudi, 'my husband and I just moved into this apartment two weeks ago.' 'Then, be careful,' warned the policeman, 'There are gangs in the neighborhood.'

When I arrived home that evening, Trudi recounted what the policeman had said about the gangs. 'But I haven't noticed any gangs,' she said. 'What gangs is he talking about?' I walked with her over to the window that overlooked the center of the complex (the one from which the policeman said that my wife could have seen the shooting) and pointed to a group of six teenagers playing cards on the sidewalk. 'I think that group of guys might be a gang.'

'But we know them!' countered Trudi, and proceeded to name all six. 'We just had them over on Friday night for pizza and a movie!'

As it turns out, a young naïve couple (us) had invited most of a gang for pizza with the hope of sharing the good news with them! We became fast friends with the whole gang from that day forward. They became our personal security. More importantly, in our invitation, we may have welcomed Christ.

Paul recounts to the Christians of southern Galatia that when he first came to their region, he was suffering from a difficult physical ailment (Gal. 4:13). Not only was he suffering, but his infirmity was of such a nature that the Galatians could have despised him for it. Nevertheless, Paul fondly remembers the way they welcomed him: 'though my condition was a trial to you, you did not scorn or despise me, but received me as an angel of God, as Christ Jesus' (Gal. 4:14). Paul wanted to encourage the Galatians by reminding them that when they received him as a stranger in distress, it was as though they welcomed an angel, or better yet, Christ Himself.

Would your attitude toward a stranger change if you thought that the person standing in front of you was actually an angel, one of God's powerful messengers, in disguise (Heb. 13:2)? I dare say it would. What if you thought that the person before you was one of your Christian friends who had secretly disguised himself as someone in need, just to see what you would do? What if you thought that maybe, just maybe, you were actually talking to Jesus?

The truth is that when you welcome someone in need, whether a sick person like Paul, or a lonely teenager who needs a friend, or a homeless person, or even an accidental gang member, you never know who you might be welcoming. It just might be Christ. It's good to keep that in mind. If the one before you is a Christian, as Paul was when he suddenly showed up as a suffering stranger in Galatia, then in some mysterious way you may actually be welcoming Christ, since that person, like Paul, is one who is *in Christ*.

CHAPTER 86

SPEAKING IN CHRIST

'For we are not, like so many, peddlers of God's word, but as men of sincerity, as commissioned by God, in the sight of God we speak in Christ' (2 Cor. 2:17).

'Have you been thinking all along that we have been defending ourselves to you? It is in the sight of God that we have been speaking in Christ, and all for your upbuilding, beloved' (2 Cor. 12:19).

'since you seek proof that Christ is speaking in me' (2 Cor. 13:3).

'Preach the gospel at all times; when necessary, use words.' How many (hundreds of!) times have you heard that line rolled out? The good part about that alleged saying of Francis of Assisi is that we need to communicate clearly that we truly believe the gospel through what we do. People should see the truth of the gospel in our lives in addition to hearing it from our mouths. But there are two problems with the way this quote is normally employed. First, it is often quoted by people who are so oriented toward social concern that they are uncomfortable with verbally proclaiming the death and resurrection of Jesus Christ and faith in Him alone. Such hesitancy to verbally share the good news of Christ simply will not do if you count yourself a biblical Christian. Second, Francis apparently never said it.

Mark Galli, who wrote a whole biography on the life of Francis, commented:

> This saying is carted out whenever someone wants to suggest that Christians *talk about* the gospel too much, and *live* the gospel too little. Fair enough—that can be a problem. Much of the

rhetorical power of the quotation comes from the assumption that Francis not only said it but lived it. The problem is that he did not say it. Nor did he live it. And those two contra-facts tell us something about the spirit of our age.[25]

As for the Apostle Paul, there can be no doubt that he believed in the importance of speaking the gospel in addition to showing the validity of the message in the way he lived. But even more, Paul cared that all verbal communication of any kind be done *in Christ*.

Notice that when Paul wrote about speaking *in Christ*, he was once writing about proclaiming the gospel to those who did not know it (2 Cor. 2:17), and twice about teaching Christians (2 Cor. 12:19; 13:3). This implies that speaking *in Christ* is shorthand for any speaking ministry, as long as it is done in connection to and dependence upon Christ. But regardless of the recipient, speaking about Christ should always be done in conscious awareness that the speaker is in relationship with Christ, trusts in Christ for the words he utters, and depends on Christ for the results.

Do you make an effort to share Christ's way of salvation with those who have never heard? Stay aware that you are connected to Christ as you speak. Do you regularly lead a small group at your church? The words that come out of your mouth should be uttered in dependence upon Christ. Do you preach or teach? Be mindful that Christ wants to communicate His message through you. Even if the only speaking God has called you to do is one-on-one, whether with Christians or non-Christians, you should be attentive to the fact that the words that come out of your mouth should agree with your *inChristness*.

Perhaps we can close this meditation by altering that so-very-popular saying (that Francis, apparently, never uttered). Here's a replacement that is certainly less catchy, but matches the Bible better: Preach the gospel at all times both to non-Christians and Christians, and since speaking is necessary, remember that your speaking must be done *in Christ*.

CHAPTER 87

LETTERS FROM CHRIST

'Are we beginning to commend ourselves again? Or do we need, as some do, letters of recommendation to you, or from you? You yourselves are our letter of recommendation, written on our hearts, to be known and read by all. And you show that you are a letter from Christ delivered by us, written not with ink but with the Spirit of the living God, not on tablets of stone but on tablets of human hearts' (2 Cor. 3:1-3).

In my day job as a college professor, one thing that takes a lot of time is writing recommendations for my students. I write recommendation letters for graduate studies, for scholarships, for study-abroad programs, for potential employers, and for mission opportunities. Letters of recommendation are an important part of the process; they help the decision-makers choose whether they should accept an application or set it aside. But one thing all these letters have in common is that the requester wants to be assured that the recommendation letter is genuine; that is, that the applicant hasn't forged a letter on his or her own behalf.

Now let's imagine a scenario where recommendation letters play a role. Suppose that you uprooted your life and moved to a distant city with the goal of planting a new church. Despite some setbacks, you led a few people to Christ, organized them into a church, appointed leaders, and finally, after a couple of years, moved on to do it again somewhere else. But after your departure you began to hear reports about outsiders who wormed their way into the group by flashing bogus letters of recommendation. How happy would you be about that?

Take it a step further. Suppose that those troublemakers accused *you* of not bringing proper letters of recommendation when you first came. You'd probably respond: 'Seriously? You need recommendation letters from me? You know me. I led you to Christ myself. *You* yourselves are my letter of recommendation. I don't need a recommendation from anyone; Christ already wrote it—on your hearts. Anyone can look at your lives and see that the message of Christ I preached to you is written on you; it can be read by everyone!'

What I have just described happened to the Apostle Paul, and led to his outburst in 2 Corinthians 3:1-3. He led people to Christ in Corinth, organized a church with local leaders, and then, after his departure, started hearing about troublemakers who touted fake letters of recommendation in an attempt to persuade the new Christ-followers to listen to *them* instead of to Paul.

Paul responded to this report by insisting that the Corinthians themselves were the only letter of recommendation he would ever need. But he didn't claim that the letter—their changed lives—was written by him. Paul would never allege something like that. He contended that it was *Christ* who wrote the letter of their lives. Paul was only the letter-carrier. Paul further asserted that everyone else could see that Christ had written His recommendation letter on their lives. Why were they having such trouble seeing it themselves?

There is something profound to take away from this interaction. Like the Corinthians, our lives are letters from Christ for everyone to read. We need to remember that people are reading our lives. But this makes me wonder… What are people reading when they look at your life? Are they reading a letter overflowing with the love of Christ? Are they coming to know what God wants to communicate about His character and purposes? Are they viewing God's message stamped on your heart? When people look at you—the way you talk, the way you live, and the way you love—is it obvious to them that you are God's letters *in Christ?*

CHAPTER 88

CREATED IN CHRIST FOR GOOD WORKS

'For we are his workmanship, created in Christ Jesus for good works, which God prepared beforehand, that we should walk in them' (Eph. 2:10).

How will people remember you when you die? Will they say that you were full of good works? Did you know that *in Christ* you were created for good works?

Think of Tabitha in the book of Acts, whom some people called Dorcas. The Bible says that she was 'full of good works and acts of charity.' When she passed away, all the widows in the area kept 'weeping and showing tunics and other garments that Dorcas made while she was with them' (Acts 9:36, 39).

Think of Barnabas, who was willing to risk his own reputation among the apostles in Jerusalem in order to introduce them to Saul (that is, Paul), the former persecutor of the church now turned believer. Acts 9:26-27 relates that when Saul came to Jerusalem: 'he attempted to join the disciples. And they were all afraid of him, for they did not believe that he was a disciple. But Barnabas took him and brought him to the apostles and declared to them how on the road he had seen the Lord, who spoke to him, and how at Damascus he had preached boldly in the name of Jesus.'

Think of Mary Magdalene, Joanna, and Susanna. As Jesus traveled from town to town preaching the good news of the kingdom of God, He not only took along His twelve disciples, there were 'also some women who had been healed of evil spirits and infirmities: Mary, called Magdalene, from whom seven demons had gone out, and Joanna, the wife of Chuza, Herod's household manager, and Susanna, and many others, who provided for them out of their means' (Luke 8:2-3). Those three women were so thankful for what Jesus had done in their lives that they responded in good works by taking care of the financial and practical needs of Jesus during His preaching tour.

Finally, think of the mother of Rufus in Rome (or, if you've never heard of her, think of her for the first time). When Paul sends greetings at the end of his letter to the Romans, he writes: 'Greet Rufus, chosen in the Lord; also his mother, who has been a mother to me as well' (Rom. 16:13). At some point during Paul's difficult life, he probably needed a stand-in mother. If Paul was willing to call Rufus's mom 'a mother to me as well' in a public letter like Romans, she must have showered Paul with heaps of love, good counsel, a warm place to sleep, and, best of all, pizza! (It was Italy, after all...)

'For we are his workmanship, created in Christ Jesus for good works, which God prepared beforehand, that we should walk in them' (Eph. 2:10). Paul writes these words immediately after his famous comment about our being saved by grace through faith, not of works, but as a gift of God (Eph. 2:8-9). God's free gift of salvation should lead to good works. We are not saved by works—Paul states this emphatically. But God purposed spiritually to recreate us in Christ so that we might display our new life in Christ by doing good works.

How will people remember you after you die? Will you be remembered for tutoring students with learning challenges? For caring for people during times of crisis? For keeping your church facilities clean and accessible and safe? For building wheelchair-accessible ramps and the like without cost? (I know someone who built just such a ramp this week.) For fostering youth who would otherwise get lost in the social system? Will you be remembered as someone through whom the grace of God overflowed into acts of service toward others? We are God's workmanship, created for good works *in Christ*.

CHAPTER 89

POWER AND WISDOM OF GOD IN CHRIST

'For Jews demand signs and Greeks seek wisdom, but we preach Christ crucified, a stumbling block to Jews and folly to Gentiles, but to those who are called, both Jews and Greeks, Christ the power of God and the wisdom of God' (1 Cor. 1:22-24).

'And because of him you are in Christ Jesus, who became to us wisdom from God' (1 Cor. 1:30).

'And I was with you in weakness and in fear and much trembling, and my speech and my message were not in plausible words of wisdom, but in demonstration of the Spirit and of power, so that your faith might not rest in the wisdom of men but in the power of God' (1 Cor. 2:3-5).

During Jesus's earthly ministry, Jewish leaders repeatedly demanded public miracles from Him to substantiate His claim that He spoke for God (Matt. 16:1; Mark 8:11; Luke 11:16; John 2:18; 6:30). Paul tersely describes this appeal for miracles with three words: 'Jews demand signs' (1 Cor. 1:22).

Then Paul adds, 'and Greeks seek wisdom' (1 Cor. 1:22). In the first century, people in the Greek-speaking world clamored to hear public speakers. Persuasive orators were the rock stars of cities like Corinth and Athens. Crowds flocked to hear them. The sophists made people laugh, cry, groan, explode in anger, and shout victory slogans. Unlike the Greek philosophers you learned about in middle school—some of whom really did seek for wisdom—these public orators only appeared wise to the crowds because of how effective they were as public communicators.

The bad news for the Apostle Paul was that he didn't measure up to the expectations of some Christians in Corinth. Though God sometimes did miracles through Paul (1 Cor. 2:4), he often appeared weak to them. That's one of the reasons the Corinthians were susceptible to false teachers; they were enamored with eloquent speakers, and clamored after miracles.

How vulnerable are you to the enticements of persuasive speakers and those claiming to be miracle-workers? I know someone who hungrily feeds on radio preachers, but has little discernment regarding the messages he ingests. 'But he's such a good speaker!' he pushes back whenever challenged to be more discerning. Years ago I had a friend who would rearrange his schedule to attend 'revival' meetings, wherever they happened to pop up, especially if lots of miracles were purportedly occurring in those meetings. 'I feel the power of God when I'm there!' he would push back whenever challenged to be more discerning.

Persuasive speakers and miracle-workers have always hovered around the Christian movement. What's wrong with that? Isn't wisdom part of the Christian life? Isn't power?

Yes, both wisdom and power are ours in Christ. But remember that any wisdom worth calling 'wisdom' and any true power you possess are inherently linked to your union with Christ. If you really are a Christian, 'you are in Christ Jesus, who became to us wisdom from God' (1 Cor. 1:30). Never lose sight of the truth of 'Christ the power of God and the wisdom of God' (1 Cor. 1:24). Don't hanker after the most demonstrative speaker or obsess over the local miracle-worker. Remember your connection to Christ, the One who was crucified in your place (1 Cor. 2:2) 'so that your faith might not rest in the wisdom of men but in the power of God' (1 Cor. 2:5).

Yes, we should seek for true wisdom, and indeed, we should claim the power we have in Christ. But we can only take hold of God's true wisdom and power by remembering our connection to our crucified and risen Christ. The power and wisdom of God—the *real* power and wisdom, not the fake kind—is ours only because we are *in Christ*.

CHAPTER 90

OPEN DOORS IN CHRIST

> 'When I came to Troas to preach the gospel of Christ, even though a door was opened for me in the Lord my spirit was not at rest' (2 Cor. 2:12-13a).
>
> 'But I will stay in Ephesus until Pentecost, for a wide door for effective work has opened to me, and there are many adversaries' (1 Cor. 16:9).
>
> 'At the same time, pray also for us, that God may open to us a door for the word, to declare the mystery of Christ, on account of which I am in prison' (Col. 4:3).

Not every door that appears to be open is an open door. And not every door that appears to be closed is a closed door. Just because a ministry setting looks like it's going to be hard doesn't mean that it is a closed door.

For the Apostle Paul, an open door was a God-given opportunity to spread the good news about Jesus. He mentioned to the Corinthians that God had opened ministry doors for him in Ephesus and Troas and requested the Colossians to pray for an open door to get the gospel out in Rome.

Perhaps the most common misunderstanding about open doors is the assumption that an open door won't be accompanied by opposition—that everything will fall neatly into place. In fact, an open door is an opportunity for the gospel to go out, but it *does not* entail the absence of hardship. Each of the three times Paul mentions open doors, hardship is there as well. In 1 Corinthians 16:9, Paul writes that he wants to stay around in Ephesus 'for a wide door for effective work has opened to me,' but immediately adds, 'and there are many adversaries.' When Paul writes that a door was open in Troas for the proclamation of the gospel, he painfully recalls that he couldn't find rest in his spirit because Titus wasn't with him (2 Cor. 2:12). And when he asks the Colossians to pray that God would 'open to us a door for the word,' he is in prison, probably awaiting trial in Rome (Col. 4:3). Just because a door is open doesn't mean that it's going to be easy.

A couple years after Trudi and I moved to the Middle East, we started praying about spearheading a new work in an unreached city where there was no gospel witness. At first we didn't tell anyone that we were praying about such a move. But we soon shared it with two godly women who began to pray along with us about this possibility, then with others who shared the same general vision and worked in similar ministries around the country. All of these prayer partners confirmed that there was an open door for ministry in our target city. But as word of our anticipated moved started to get out, some believers around the country began to spread negative comments. 'That is a really religious city.' 'The spiritual warfare there is intense.' And even, 'You'll be lucky to last a year.'

So, was there a wide-open door for ministry or not? Yes, there was. And yet, there were also many adversaries. The naysayers were correct, at least in some ways. We did face periods living in that city when life was truly difficult. But God did establish a spiritual presence there, notwithstanding many trials because, in fact, a wide-open door for ministry did exist there.

Is there a ministry into which you think God may want you to step? Does that ministry look like it might be difficult? Let me remind you that if you see potential for God's Word to take root and blossom— even if there is potential for adversity—it could still be an open door *in Christ*.

CHAPTER 91

FRAGRANCE OF CHRIST

> 'For we are the aroma of Christ to God among those who are being saved and among those who are perishing, to one a fragrance from death to death, to the other a fragrance from life to life. Who is sufficient for these things?' (2 Cor. 2:15-16).

One smell you'll probably never encounter on the streets of Los Angeles where I live, but that is common in Iran, Azerbaijan, Greece, Turkey, and the Balkans is the smell of rotisserie Kokoretsi (Greek spelling). Kokoretsi looks like a wound-up ball of rope that someone decided to cook. That's because it *is* a long rope—of animal intestines. Honestly, I can't stand the smell of Kokoretsi, but I know plenty of people whose mouths start to water the moment a waft of the stuff comes in contact with their olfactory nerves. You might say that Kokoretsi is 'to one a fragrance from death to death, to the other a fragrance from life to life' (2 Cor. 2:16). Same smell, different response.

What do people smell when they smell you? If you are in *Christ*—and you are if you truly know Christ—some people will *like* the way you smell and be drawn to your message, while others will be repelled by it.

I'm thinking of a well-known athlete who openly acknowledges that he is a Christ-follower. He is not at all pushy, mind you, just unashamed to tell others that he belongs to Christ. A lot of Christians appreciate his Christian testimony. Some who normally don't follow sports support him simply because they're glad for a positive representative of their faith. On the other hand, the amount of public vitriol that has been spewed against this young man—simply because he is unafraid to acknowledge that he is a believer in Christ—has been excessive. Same message...same fragrance...varying responses.

Perhaps now is a good time to clear up a misconception. I know some Christians who think that if we could just package our message in an inoffensive way, people would automatically come to faith. They suppose that if we could only figure out how to manufacture the precise formula for our fragrance, people would inevitably be drawn to the pleasant scent. In other words, they think that the only problem with people coming to faith is the bad odor Christians put off.

I'm afraid that people who think this way are a bit naïve. While I wholeheartedly agree that we should strive to remove anything that hinders people from receiving the message of the gospel (as long as the gospel itself is not altered in any way), and while I enthusiastically agree that we should seek to become all things to all people to win some (1 Cor. 9:22), we need to remember that the gospel will always be a stumbling block to some and foolishness to others (1 Cor. 1:23). Some people will refuse to accept the message no matter how well it is packaged.

Still, just because some will be drawn to the fragrance of Christ in you while others are repelled by it doesn't give you permission to be inconsiderate or pushy or arrogant when talking to those who don't believe. You should seek for your scent to match your message, a message about reconciliation through Christ. In other words, don't dilute the fragrant message of Christ with a putrid odor that hinders people from accepting the message.

Oh that our lives might emit the fragrance of Christ! May people be drawn to Jesus through our lives the way I am irresistibly drawn to the smell of fresh bread! But even if we are careful not to dilute the message, some people will never be able to smell the wonderful aroma of Christ since they have chosen death over life. This too, is part of what it means to be *in Christ*.

CHAPTER 92

CONTROLLED BY THE LOVE OF CHRIST

'the in-Christ-Jesus love' (1 Tim. 1:14; 2 Tim. 1:13 literal translation).

'For the love of Christ controls us' (2 Cor. 5:14).

Jeremiah, the prophet-of-pain, once wrote, 'If I say, "I will not mention him, or speak any more in his name," there is in my heart as it were a burning fire shut up in my bones, and I am weary with holding it in, and I cannot' (Jer. 20:9). Jeremiah could not contain the message entrusted to him. He had to share it.

A fire also burned in the heart of the Apostle Paul. That fire was the *love of Christ* (2 Cor. 5:14). Paul said that it *controlled* him. *Constrained* him. *Impelled* him. *Urged* him to do what he did. Modern translators have used all these words in attempts to approximate Paul's intention. The verb in this context may carry a dual meaning: the idea of control (that is, guarding Paul from self-love), and the idea of pressing him into service (compelling him to act, urging him forward). Paul was constrained by the love of Christ to persuade others to be reconciled to Christ (2 Cor. 5:11, 18-20). It gave Paul direction and moved him forward. There was only one way Paul could respond to such extravagant love: he had to share it.

But what did Paul mean by 'the love of Christ'? Syntactically, this little expression can mean either 'Christ's love for us' or 'our love for Christ.' Which is it? Is Paul saying that he has been so overcome with Christ's sacrificial love that he is constrained to do what he does, as the following expression might suggest ('because...one died for all' [2 Cor. 5:14])? Or should we focus on Paul's zeal for Christ that reverberates through all the chapters surrounding this verse, which would support the second idea: that Paul does what he does because he passionately loves Christ? I have spent years thinking about this question. I am now persuaded that somehow both Christ's love for us and our love for Christ are involved in this little expression in this verse.[26] Paul was motivated by Christ's love for him *and* compelled by his love for Christ. Paul was so moved by Christ's sacrificial death, and appropriately responded in cut-loose love for Christ, that he—as a result of the giving-and-receiving love fest between him and his Lord—was constrained, controlled, and compelled to take the love of Christ to the world.

What motivates you? Are you stirred merely by a sense of duty, that as a good Christian you ought to reach out to your neighbors and co-workers with the gospel? Or have you been really and truly engaged by the love of Christ? Everything looks different when you serve others out of a response to the lavish love of Christ. Your perspective gets appropriately altered and you become so occupied with loving Christ that your actions increasingly are driven forward by that love. Every part of your being gets impacted when you live your life out of a loving relationship with the One who loved you more than life itself. Receiving and responding. Accepting and admiring. Loving and being loved…and loving and being loved again…and loving and being loved again. Then turning that love outward to share the love of Christ with a world that is dying for love.

It's true, the world is dying for love, but we have an answer for that longing. Are you so taken with the love of Christ that you are compelled to share it with others? Will you tell them—controlled by the love of Christ—that they can be united with Christ by faith; that they, too, like you can be *in Christ*?

CHAPTER 93

RECONCILIATION THROUGH CHRIST

'All this is from God, who through Christ reconciled us to himself and gave us the ministry of reconciliation; that is, in Christ God was reconciling the world to himself, not counting their trespasses against them, and entrusting to us the message of reconciliation' (2 Cor. 5:18-19).

One of my favorite sub-plots in the story of Paul is his relationship with John Mark, probably the same Mark who authored the Gospel of Mark.

When Barnabas and Paul embarked on their first missionary journey, they invited Mark, Barnabas's cousin (Col. 4:10), to assist them in their outreach (Acts 12:25; 13:5). Mark served with Barnabas and Paul on the island of Cyprus, then sailed with them toward the mainland of what is today southern Turkey. There Mark deserted them (Acts 13:13). Was there a disagreement of some sort? Was John Mark afraid of persecution they might encounter on the mainland? No one knows for sure. But while Paul and Barnabas shared the gospel and suffered together (Acts 13-14), Mark wasn't with them.

So a couple years later when Paul and Barnabas decided to embark on a second missionary journey, and Barnabas suggested that they invite cousin Mark to accompany them—you know, give him a second chance—Paul pushed back. 'And there arose a sharp disagreement, so that they separated from each other' (Acts 15:39). Barnabas took Mark and left for Cyprus. Paul stayed a bit longer in Antioch, selected Silas as his ministry partner, then set out after being commended to the ministry by the church in Antioch (Acts 15:36-41).

That was it. Mark had separated the dynamic duo, Paul and Barnabas. Don't forget that this occurred in an honor-and-shame culture. Mark was the cause of a rift between Barnabas and Paul. In their cultural context, there was no going back. Paul and Mark's relationship was finished. Or was it?

No, in fact, it wasn't. Paul and Mark reconciled—really reconciled. A decade later, we find Paul under house arrest in Rome writing one letter to the Colossian church and one to a member of the Colossian church named Philemon. Who do you suppose is with Paul? Yes, Mark (Col. 4:10). Not only is he with him, he is one of Paul's ministry partners (Philem. 24). But a far more touching comment is found in Paul's final written words penned a few years later just before his martyrdom. Paul wrote to Timothy, 'Luke alone is with me. Get Mark and bring him with you, for he is very useful to me for ministry' (2 Tim. 4:11).

How did this happen? How on earth in an honor-and-shame society could Paul and Mark reconcile—not only forgive each other, but reunite so completely that they ended up working together in a ministry of reconciliation? The answer is suggested in 2 Corinthians 5:18-19. Paul—and certainly Mark as well—had personally owned the truth that 'through Christ' God 'reconciled us to himself and gave us the ministry of reconciliation; that is, in Christ God was reconciling the world to himself, not counting their trespasses against them, and entrusting to us the message of reconciliation.'

They knew that God had brought them into a close relationship with Himself through the work of Christ, and that God had thereby entrusted to them the message that others could be reconciled to God. Everyone who has been reconciled to God in Christ is a minister of reconciliation to others ('reconciled *us*' and 'gave *us*' this ministry). Paul and Mark were reunited with each other against all cultural odds, and worked together to invite others to be united to Christ. They reconciled with one another and called others to the same because they knew that they had first been reconciled to God *in Christ.*

CHAPTER 94

AMBASSADORS FOR CHRIST

> 'Therefore, we are ambassadors for Christ, God making his appeal through us. We implore you on behalf of Christ, be reconciled to God' (2 Cor. 5:20).

It turns out that I have one somewhat famous ancestor (apart from Adam and Noah). I am a direct descendant of John Hart, one of the signers of the *Declaration of Independence* of the United States of America. Hart's is the second-to-last signature on the fourth column at the bottom of the document, just in case you decide to look for it!

John Hart was an 'ambassador,' if we borrow the wording of 2 Corinthians 5:20. He represented New Jersey at the Second Continental Congress and ratified the *Declaration* on behalf of that state. Hart suffered considerably for his representative mission. Within months of signing, British and mercenary troops ransacked Hart's property in New Jersey. His wife took ill and died, possibly as a result of injuries incurred during attacks on the family property. Hart himself hid in forests and caves for more than a month trying to elude loyalist troops who hunted him. His role as a representative of New Jersey was costly.

'We are ambassadors for Christ.' Technically, the word 'ambassadors' in Greek is not a noun; it's a verb. The emphasis lies more upon what we do, not on a title we possess. In other words, we are *ambassador-ing* on behalf of Christ. An obvious implication is that we shouldn't call ourselves ambassadors unless we are actually doing the work of *ambassador-ing*.

What are some characteristics of ambassadors?

1. Ambassadors represent someone other than themselves. This means that if we are ambassadors of Christ, we must seek to represent Him well.

2. Ambassadors are sent on a mission. Our job, according to 2 Corinthians 5:20, is to appeal to others to be reconciled to God through Jesus Christ. Our appeal is not *our* appeal, but is 'on Christ's behalf' and 'as though God were making his appeal through us' (NIV).

3. Ambassadors sometimes suffer as a consequence of their connection to their sender. Jesus said, 'If they persecuted me, they will also persecute you' (John 15:20). Paul suffered numerous indignities as an ambassador of Christ; his sufferings pepper the pages of 2 Corinthians (see chapters 1, 4, 6, 11). We shouldn't be surprised if we face opposition, or, in some cases, even persecution, for seeking to represent a crucified Savior.

Do you have neighbors? Most people I know, except for those living 'off the grid,' have neighbors! Can your neighbors tell from the way you conduct yourself that you are an ambassador for Christ? (They are watching you through their windows, you know!) Are they able to figure out that you are Christ's ambassador from the way you speak to them? Wait, you never speak to your neighbors? Well, that's a different kind of problem...

Do you have any work associates or classmates with whom you interact on a daily, or even weekly, basis? If someone were to ask one of those friends or work associates about you, would at least part of their description include your connection to Jesus? Do they observe, even if they don't know anything about Christian *ambassador-ing,* that you earnestly seek to represent Jesus Christ in what you say and do? If they know that you claim to be a Christ-follower, do your words coincide with your actions?

The world desperately needs to be reconciled to God. God has opened a way to reconciliation through the death and resurrection of Jesus. As believers in Jesus, we have already received our reconciliation. As disciples of Jesus, we have been sent on a mission to share this reconciliation. We are ambassadors of Christ, carrying a message of reconciliation with God through Jesus Christ, as people *in Christ.*

CHAPTER 95

FOOLS FOR CHRIST

'If anyone among you thinks that he is wise in this age, let him become a fool that he may become wise' (1 Cor. 3:18).

'Already you have all you want! Already you have become rich! Without us you have become kings! And would that you did reign, so that we might share the rule with you! For I think that God has exhibited us apostles as last of all, like men sentenced to death, because we have become a spectacle to the world, to angels, and to men. We are fools for Christ's sake' (1 Cor. 4:8-10).

Fools for Christ? Like the time my emergency alarm went off inside my suitcase as it slid into the baggage carousel at Los Angeles International Airport and I suddenly found myself surrounded by airport police? Or the time I unknowingly sat down in the middle of a chapel filled with 1,000 students, and looked up to discover it was a girls' only chapel? Or the time I forgot to turn off my teaching microphone when I went to the restroom?

Nobody likes to feel foolish. Nobody wants to be the object of others' ridicule. But identifying with Christ will sometimes cause us to appear foolish in the eyes of others. There's no way around it.

Paul and his fellow missionaries were viewed as foolish by some in Corinth. The problem wasn't with Paul; it was with the distorted picture of the Christian life the Corinthians had imbibed from false teachers, and that was now getting imposed upon Paul. These new believers assumed that since they were God's children, they should receive abundant blessings by God in the present age. If their future destiny was to rule, they thought they should live like kings now. If crowns awaited them in the future, they had the right to receive riches now. If they would one day be free from suffering and sickness, they should be healed now.

In contrast to this skewed vision of the Christian life, Paul and his ministry team appeared foolish. The Corinthians who had accepted such teaching simply couldn't grasp how Paul could be a true apostle of Christ and yet encounter constant setbacks, sorrow, and suffering. What a fool to undergo hardship when it was all so unnecessary!

Have you ever been viewed as foolish because of your belief that Christ is worthy of your whole self? Someone you work with says he doesn't mind if you want to believe whatever you want on your own time, but 'why does everything have to revolve around Jesus?' An unbelieving family member can't fathom why you give so much money to missions, commenting on the 'waste.'

But it isn't only unbelievers who view you as foolish. Sometimes people who claim allegiance to Christ do the same. That's what Paul faced from some of the Christians in Corinth. For example, the Christian woman you regularly meet for coffee tells you she's tired of hearing so much God-talk; youth group friends don't want to hang around you because 'you're just too…Christian'; even your Christian spouse thinks you might 'need to cool off a bit.'

What I am *not* saying is that we should be foolish in the way we talk about our Christian faith. We may not always be able to avoid being viewed as foolish by those who don't understand our relationship to Christ, but we should not insensitively impose unloving, unkind, or unthoughtful words on others, whether they know Christ or not. Still, we who have died to our old lives, entered into new life, and seek to live out our faith in Christ in word and deed will inevitably be viewed as foolish by some. We can willingly embrace our status as fools for Christ because we are connected to Christ, and derive our status as 'fools' because we are *in Christ.*

CHAPTER 96

SPIRITUAL WARFARE IN CHRIST

> 'Finally, be strong in the Lord and in the strength of his might. Put on the whole armor of God, that you may be able to stand against the schemes of the devil. For we do not wrestle against flesh and blood, but against the rulers, against the authorities, against the cosmic powers over this present darkness, against the spiritual forces of evil in the heavenly places' (Eph. 6:10-12).

Spiritual warfare is real. This is the case whether or not you spend time thinking about it. Nor does it disappear if you try not to think about it. Just as you can't stop someone from committing a crime by closing your eyes, neither can you halt spiritual warfare by pretending it isn't there.

What is spiritual warfare? Paul defines it as wrestling against the spiritual forces of evil in the heavenly places (Eph. 6:12). More directly, the Bible teaches that there is a real devil—a powerful angel (Satan)—who sinned in the past along with other powerful angels (demons). This powerful evil being is intent on preventing God's kingdom work in the world. This means that if you are leaning into the truth that you can 'be strong *in the Lord* and in the strength of his might,' you will sometimes face attacks. Satan and his army of demons will try to stop you. Tempt you. Spread dissension among your brothers and sisters. Attack your health. Mess with your plumbing.

Trudi and I have been facing spiritual warfare for the past three weeks (at the time I'm writing this chapter). We prayed for more than twenty years that God would provide a way for us to start a small live-in Christian community with college students for the purpose of discipleship. Seven weeks ago (at this writing), we moved into our new community—three living spaces on one property—with the possibility of housing as many as ten college students (in separate apartments) plus our family.

As a result, we have a target on our back. The spiritual forces of evil aren't happy with what we're trying to do. They also know that one of our spiritual weak-points is plumbing. So in the past month, we've had a water heater give out, a garbage disposal freeze up, a sewage cap pop off in the crawl space under our house (I'll spare you the details), water leak into our house from two different windows during a rainstorm, and a complex drainage problem emerge in our garage. Am I certain that this is spiritual warfare and not simply water problems? No. But I've experienced similar occurrences frequently enough in the past to remind me of the possibility—likelihood even—that we are facing spiritual opposition as a result of our foray into a new ministry.

But what does *inChristness* have to do with facing spiritual attack? Ephesians 6:10 instructs us to 'be strong *in the Lord* and in the strength of his might.' I can resist the devil only because I am *in Christ*. Otherwise, my power is inadequate. I know that the Lord Jesus announced the defeat of Satan and his demons at the cross (Col. 2:15). Because I am united with Christ, I have the right to claim victory over the Evil One. God may (and sometimes does) allow him to attack me—or my plumbing! But Satan cannot and will not ultimately prevail against God's child, because a son or daughter of God is *in Christ*.

Everything else you need to know about how to deal with spiritual warfare (prayer, Scripture, taking authority) starts and ends with holding fast to the truth that you have been united to Christ. What then? Paul exclaims: 'having done all, to stand firm' (Eph. 6:13). 'Stand therefore...' (Eph. 6:14) not in your own strength, but because you are *in Christ*.

CHAPTER 97

PERSECUTION IN CHRIST

'my imprisonment is for Christ' (Phil. 1:13).

'Paul, a prisoner for Christ Jesus' (Eph. 3:1; Philem. 1, 9).

'Epaphras, my fellow prisoner in Christ Jesus' (Philem. 23).

'Indeed, all who desire to live a godly life in Christ Jesus will be persecuted' (2 Tim. 3:12).

It was my final meal with my students. These were not, however, American Christian college students. I had just finished teaching a twelve-day crash course in Biblical Greek to forty Russian, Ukrainian, and Belarusian pastors and church leaders in Kyiv, Ukraine. Eight hours a day they studied Greek—and I taught through a Russian translator! My new friends acquired Greek far more quickly than American students typically do. This was probably because East Slavic languages, including Russian, Ukrainian, and Belarusian, are case-based languages like Greek, so when I started talking about nominatives, genitives, datives, and accusatives, they already had a good idea of what I was talking about.

I had grown to love these students over shared meals, extra tutoring sessions, and games of volleyball. As we played and laughed together, it was easy to forget that some of them had suffered for their faith under the oppressive regimes of the Soviet Union. But I will never forget my students' parting gift, a memory I will treasure for the rest of my life, and even now produces tears as I write these words. As we finished our meal, one of the older students announced that all the students wanted to sing a song as a parting gift to me. But first he explained the story behind the song.

More than eighty years previously, as Stalin's iron grip closed around Russia, one of the most brutal persecutions of Christians in the history of the world was unleashed. When twelve pastors applied to attend the

Fourth Baptist World Congress in Toronto, Canada in June of 1928, they were granted permission to attend, but were warned that if any uttered a word about the crackdown on Christians, their families back in Russia would suffer for it.

So when those pastors showed up at the conference, they were unable to say anything about the dreadful persecution expanding daily against Christians in Russia under Stalin's regime. Instead, those men stood before the delegates in Canada and sang in Russian the same mournful song that my students stood and sang for me on our final day together (here in translation):

Wildly life's billows 'round my soul are beating
Fierce is the tempest, dangerous is the sea
Driven by terror, I come to you, pleading
'Father in heaven, O hear Thou my plea!'

In Thy great mercy, help me, I implore Thee
Long have I struggled, but to no avail
My strength is spent—I cast myself before Thee
'Help me, my Father, without Thee I fail!'

Into the calmness of Thy harbour guide me
Instill a peace and trust within my soul
Amid life's tempest stay Thou o'er beside me
Bring me at last to my heavenly goal.

A holy hush surrounded the room as they finished the final stanza. Everything was silent except for my muffled weeping. I later learned that one of those twelve pastors stayed in the West, while the other eleven who returned to Russia faced severe persecution for their faith, with most of them being martyred.

Please remember those brave brothers if ever you face real persecution as a Christian. Suffering for Christ is a gift (Phil. 1:29). Like those beloved Russian believers who sang that soulful yet faith-filled lament in 1928, and just like my students who reiterated that song eighty years later, you will endure as long as you remember that nothing, not even persecution and death, can ever come between you and your Lord—because you are *in Christ*.[27]

CHAPTER 98

CONFIDENCE IN CHRIST

'I want you to know, brothers, that what has happened to me has really served to advance the gospel, so that it has become known throughout the whole imperial guard and to all the rest that my imprisonment is for Christ. And most of the brothers, having become confident in the Lord by my imprisonment, are much more bold to speak the word without fear' (Phil. 1:12-14).

Have you ever been afraid to do something, but after watching someone else do it first, decided to give it a try? I was afraid to jump off a high dive at the swimming pool when I was eight years old, but after noticing that a few children of my age (and younger!) did it first, I took the leap...and lived to tell about it.

Lacking the confidence to share your faith in Jesus Christ with others is similar in one way to my fear of jumping off a high dive. Many Christians fear sharing their faith with those who do not know Christ because they have never seen anyone do it. For this reason, I have now taken hundreds of college students in small groups to share the gospel at local secular university campuses. Those students are sometimes visibly trembling on their first outreach, even though they voluntarily signed up to join me. (Full disclosure: I am sometimes afraid, too.) But when they observe me or one of their more experienced classmates entering into respectful conversations about the good news with people who really need it, their confidence increases.

But what if your environment is one of true hostility or even outright persecution? How can you gain confidence to share your faith in such a setting?

Paul explains to the Philippians that when he was imprisoned, under house arrest, and chained to a Roman guard, that many of the Christians in Rome 'having become confident in the Lord by my imprisonment, are much more bold to speak the word without fear' (Phil. 1:14).

Notice that Paul doesn't explain *how* they became confident, but we can infer how it happened. We learn from the ending of the book of Acts that although Paul was confined to a house in Rome for two years, he was permitted visitors with whom he regularly and boldly shared the gospel (Acts 28:30-31). That example alone would have bolstered the courage of the Roman Christians. But Paul didn't limit his conversations to outside visitors. He must have regularly shared the good news with the soldiers to whom he was chained twenty-four hours a day. That is how he could write in Philippians 1:13, 'so that it has become known throughout the whole imperial guard and to all the rest that my imprisonment is for Christ'. If Paul had the courage to share the gospel with soldiers who had the power to make his life miserable, the Roman Christians would have reasoned, at least I can tell my neighbor about Christ! Paul's example led to their increased confidence.

After only a couple of hours of gospel-oriented conversations, students who accompany me on outings to share their faith often comment: 'That wasn't nearly as hard as I thought it would be!' In most cases, those students have prayed their way through the entire process, depended upon the Holy Spirit to empower them, and rooted their hearts in their *inChristness,* remembering the solid position from which they have shared the message of life in Christ. Granted, their confidence gets reinforced and even increases when they observe the example of others who share their faith with confidence and grace, but it is most fundamentally sustained when they depend upon Christ. You, too, will increase in confidence in sharing your faith as you remember that you are *in Christ.*

CHAPTER 99

SOLDIERS OF CHRIST

> 'Share in suffering as a good soldier of Christ Jesus. No soldier gets entangled in civilian pursuits, since his aim is to please the one who enlisted him' (2 Tim. 2:3-4).

'Onward Christian soldiers, marching as to war. With the cross of Jesus going on before.' So reads the first line and chorus of a hymn written toward the end of the nineteenth century and that was sung *a lot* during the twentieth.[28] I grew up singing this song. If I'm honest, I have to confess that I often struggle when Christians use military metaphors to describe the Christian life. My discomfort isn't because such imagery is absent from the Bible (it isn't), but because my sensitivities regarding militaristic language—even when used metaphorically—got heightened during the years I lived in the Middle East. Due to various religious wars of the past—the Crusades in particular—Middle Easterners are touchy about Christians using religious-warfare language. They often interpret such language as references to literal military campaigns in which misguided zealots wed religious fervor with literal warfare. I understand their concerns. But literal military campaigns are not at all what Paul was writing about when he encouraged Christ-followers to view themselves as soldiers of Christ.

As Christians, we fight against Satan and his army of demons. We fight against our own natural inclinations to sin, that is, we battle the 'flesh.' We fight against injustices wherever they are found, and seek to stop evil people from hurting the vulnerable and weak. Our enemy is not other people: 'we do not wrestle against flesh and blood' (Eph. 6:12). When Paul uses military metaphors, he is thinking of fighting against the devil, against world systems that have been corrupted by evil and injustice, and against our tendencies to sin (Eph. 2:2-3).

So what are the benefits of viewing ourselves as soldiers? In 2 Timothy 2:3-4, Paul describes three aspects of soldiering that are pertinent to the Christian life:

First, soldiers willingly enter into suffering. Paul wrote: 'Share in suffering as a good soldier of Christ Jesus.' That was Paul's straightforward acknowledgment that when someone enlists, the new recruit knows up-front that he will suffer in some way. The soldier's mission will be accompanied by hardship, fatigue, injury, and possible death. When we view ourselves as soldiers of Christ Jesus, we remind ourselves of what we knew when we enlisted: soldiers of Christ sometimes suffer.

Second, soldiers avoid worldly entanglements. Paul added: 'No soldier gets entangled in civilian pursuits.' Paul warned against allowing worldly responsibilities and pleasures to distract from the mission God has commanded us to pursue. How easily distractible are you? Are you focused upon pursuing the victory of Christ at all costs, or do you get easily sidetracked?

Third, soldiers seek to please their superiors. Paul explained that a soldier avoids worldly distractions 'since his aim is to please the one who enlisted him.' When your enlisting officer (who is also your training officer and commanding officer) is Jesus Christ Himself, you can entrust yourself entirely and wholeheartedly to Him. You never have to worry that your superior might lead you astray, or abandon you during a battle, or get lost and not know where to go next. His faithfulness, steadfastness, power, and know-how will guide you through every pressure you encounter. The proper response for a soldier is the desire to please in every possible way the One who directs his mission.

In short, a soldier of Christ suffers *in Christ*, avoids worldly entanglements by living life *in Christ*, and seeks to live a God-pleasing life *in Christ*.

CHAPTER 100

MINISTRY RESULTS THROUGH CHRIST

'For I will not venture to speak of anything except what Christ has accomplished through me to bring the Gentiles to obedience—by word and deed' (Rom. 15:18).

'For this I toil, struggling with all his energy that he powerfully works within me' (Col. 1:29).

I was discouraged. I had been seeking to plant a church during the previous year-and-a-half in one of the most unreached cities on earth, but little was moving spiritually. On the contrary, I had just discovered that one of the new 'believers' was actually a *mole,* secretly collecting and feeding information about our activities to the local authorities. Moreover, there was so little spiritual movement during that period that I sometimes thanked God for the *trees*—at least *they* would one day break out in praise to God. I was far less certain that any *people* were going to praise God on the Final Day.

On this particular morning, my wife and I were participating in a camp for scattered believers who had come together for mutual encouragement from all over this difficult country. It was early morning and I was walking beside the seashore with my two-year-old daughter, Lydia. She bent over, picked up a small stone, and threw it into the water. This gave me an idea. At the precise moment she tossed her next pebble, I heaved a much larger stone over her shoulder. 'Kerplunk!' Lydia squealed in delight that *she* could produce such a splash. I secretly lobbed stone after stone into the water in unison with Lydia, creating a splash twenty times larger than she could have produced with her pebbles.

All of a sudden, I sensed the presence of God all around me. Even though I kept playing the game with my daughter, I became intensely aware that God was there. I knew there was a message here for me. 'Ken, keep tossing your little ministry pebbles, but remember, I am the only One who can make it splash. Stop acting like it's up to you. It's not. It's *my* work.' I eventually had to stop the game because my eyes were so full of tears I couldn't see straight. God ministered deeply to me in that moment. I think that even my two-year-old daughter knew something important was happening to her daddy.

I returned to the city where God had planted me, not simply renewed in my commitment to share Christ in word and deed, but far more dependent upon the Lord for spiritual results. That morning beside the sea, I embraced the truth that *all spiritual ministry* happens *through Christ*. There are lots of external ministry-goals we can set and reach—we can plan youth activities, organize conferences, canvas neighborhoods, and care for the poor, but there is *nothing spiritual that lasts* unless it is accomplished by Christ.

Can you see how freeing this is? If I believed that I could produce spiritual fruit, I would be prone to take credit when something good occurred and correspondingly carry the weight of discouragement upon my shoulders when I perceived no forward progress. But when I remember that only Christ can accomplish spiritual work, it forces me radically to trust Him to accomplish everything—even as I step out in faith. There is no space for passivity in this. God has called me to 'toil' and 'struggle' in ministry, as Colossians 1:29 clearly indicates, but I am also to do it 'with all his energy that he powerfully works within me'—which is the second part of the same verse. Then I will be able to agree with the Apostle Paul when he says, 'I will not venture to speak of anything except what Christ has accomplished through me' (Rom. 15:18).

All ministry—that is, all lasting spiritual ministry—is accomplished through Christ and *in Christ*.

BONUS CHAPTER
ABIDING IN CHRIST

One of the most important passages for understanding *inChristness* in the letters of Paul, surprisingly, is not even found in his writings. It is a passage spoken by Jesus, recorded for us by one of Jesus's disciples in John 15. Notice Jesus's use of the word 'in.'

> I am the true vine, and my Father is the vinedresser. Every branch *in* me that does not bear fruit he takes away, and every branch that does bear fruit he prunes, that it may bear more fruit. Already you are clean because of the word that I have spoken to you. Abide *in* me, and I in you. As the branch cannot bear fruit by itself, unless it abides *in* the vine, neither can you, unless you abide *in* me. I am the vine; you are the branches. Whoever abides *in* me and I *in* him, he it is that bears much fruit, for apart from me you can do nothing (John 15:1-5).

It is almost impossible to believe that the Apostle Paul wrote so much about being 'in Christ' without ever thinking about Jesus's teaching about abiding in the vine. Paul didn't make up the idea of *inChristness* at all; he learned it from Jesus.

But unlike Paul, Jesus applied a verb to help us respond to this in-Christ relationship, the verb 'abide.' Some modern translations render this Greek word (*menō*) as 'remain.' Probably the most accurate translation of this word in context I've ever come across is the Hawaiian Pidgin translation, which renders John 15:4: 'Stay tight wit' me.' That translation brings out the relational closeness inherent in Jesus's teaching in the way the word 'abide' mostly doesn't and that 'remain' doesn't at all. It is not just that you continue following Christ; rather, you live in such a tight relationship with Him that only a preposition like 'in' can approximate it.

The Apostle Paul seized hold of this; that's why he weaved *inChristness* into his writings and used the concept to connect so many major teachings. Paul remembered that Jesus was the first to tell His disciples, and disciples of all time, to stay tight with Jesus. Paul decided to apply that truth to almost everything else in the Christian life.

I had the privilege of sitting through two year-long Bible classes with Mrs. Lucille Carr during my late teens. Mrs. Carr was old. ('How old was she?' you ask. She was so old that she had served in China as a missionary *before* the communists took over China.) My friend Trudi (now my wife) used to admire all the wrinkles on Mrs. Carr's face! I knew Mrs. Carr loved me, and I gathered that she was praying for me. But now that I am all grown up, I think it likely that she also had concerns about my impulsiveness and self-confidence.

It was nearly summer break. I remember it well. Mrs. Carr wrote a private note encouraging me to spend the upcoming summer meditating on John 15.

So I did. Mrs. Carr was a godly woman, and despite my young age I recognized the wisdom in listening to the advice of a matriarch in the faith. But try as I might, I never really *got* John 15 that summer. All that vine-branch stuff was a lovely metaphor, but I knew we weren't going to change the world hanging around like branches on vines!

I'm older now. Not as old as Mrs. Carr—I don't think I'll ever be that old—but old enough to have discovered that life isn't primarily about *doing* stuff. That's what Mrs. Carr wanted me to learn. Life isn't primarily about evangelization or Bible memorization, or even obedience to Christ's commands, important as all of those are. Life is, first and foremost, an abiding relationship with a gracious and loving Lord. It is living life *in Christ.*

THANKS

I am deeply grateful for all who have walked with me through the process of writing these 100 devotional readings on the 'in Christ' life. I want to thank my immediate family members who allowed me to read aloud to them and dialogue with them about new chapters over evening meals: my life-partner Trudi, my daughters Ana, Ela, Grace, and Lydia, and my son-in-law Joshua. Robert and Davette Bishop, Linda Garcia, and Denise Felli read portions of the book and offered much-needed encouragement along the way. Many students over the past three years in my Life & Letters of Paul classes at Biola University have read sections of the book and written papers that have helped me think more deeply about what I have been writing. Three people in particular sacrificed large amounts of time to suggest edits and probe me with thoughtful questions: my father Drew Berding, my long-term friend Steve Payne, and my former student Nick Galvan. Nick also worked with me on review questions, and Barnabas Kwok compiled a Scripture index. I so appreciate them all! Finally, I want to acknowledge the tireless efforts of the editors and staff at Christian Focus Publications who have labored diligently in the Lord to bring this book into your hands. I thank God for their partnership in this ministry.

ENDNOTES

1   See, for example, Kenneth Berding, *Walking in the Spirit* (Crossway, 2011) and *What Are Spiritual Gifts? Rethinking the Conventional View* (Kregel, 2006).

2   Ephesians 1:3-14 is a good example of such a pile-up. Translators even occasionally remove the words 'into him' (εἰς αὐτόν) in the middle of verse 5 and ('in him') (ἐν αὐτῷ) at the end of verse 10 because there are so many such expressions that some translators view these as simply repetitive. But perhaps the pile-up of such expressions wasn't merely repetitive for Paul, but rather was insistently and intentionally emphatic.

3   The illustration was adapted from D. James Kennedy, *Evangelism Explosion*, 4th ed. (Wheaton, IL: Tyndale House, 1996), 42.

4   J. E. Hutton, *A History of the Moravian Church*, 2nd ed. (London: Moravian Publication Office, 1909), 234-39.

5   George Orwell, *Animal Farm* (London: Secker and Warburg, 1946).

6   Translation from Kenneth Berding, *The Apostolic Fathers: A Narrative Introduction* (Eugene, OR: Wipf & Stock, 2017), 99.

7   For more on Polycarp, see the short dictionary article: Kenneth Berding, 'Polycarp of Smyrna' in *The Encyclopedia of Ancient History*, ed. Roger Bagnall, Kai Brodersen, Craige Champion, Andrew Erskine, and Sabine Huebner (Wiley-Blackwell, 2013), 5396-97; or my academic monograph: *Polycarp and Paul: An Analysis of Their Literary & Theological Relationship in Light of Polycarp's Use of Biblical and Extra-Biblical Literature. Supplements to Vigiliae Christianae 62* (Leiden: Brill, 2002). For a general introduction to the 'apostolic fathers,' of whom Polycarp is one of the most important, see my easy-to-read introduction: *The Apostolic Fathers: A Narrative Introduction* (Eugene, OR: Wipf & Stock, 2017).

8   Marco Rubio, January 14, 2016.

9   Robert Boyd Munger, *My Heart – Christ's Home* (Downers Grove, IL: IVP Books, 1986).

10   This is a shortened retelling of Ömer Seyfettin's story *Ant*. 'Ant' is a Turkish word that translates into English as 'covenant,' 'promise,' or 'oath.' A slightly longer version in English of the same story is told by

Simon Greaves, *The Blood Brothers*, ed. Cathy Hall (Orient Structural Readers Stage 3).

11 Leon Morris, *The Epistle to the Romans* (Grand Rapids: Eerdmans and Leicester: Inter-Varsity, 1988), 246-47.

12 Donald Guthrie, *The Pastoral Epistles*, rev. ed., Tyndale New Testament Commentaries (Leicester: InterVarsity and Grand Rapids: Eerdmans, 1990), 149.

13 For a helpful explanation of this, see Thomas R. Schreiner, *Paul: Apostle of God's Glory in Christ: A Pauline Theology* (Downers Grove: InterVarsity and Leicester: Apollos, 2001): 57-60.

14 John Reumann, *Philippians, The Anchor Yale Bible* (New Haven and London: Yale University Press, 2008), 557-558 (also 550-551).

15 Frances Jane (Fanny) Crosby, 'He Hideth My Soul,' in *The Finest of Wheat, No. 1* (Chicago, IL: R. R. McCabe, 1890). Music by William James Kirkpatrick.

16 Murray J. Harris, *The Second Epistle to the Corinthians: A Commentary on the Greek Text* (Grand Rapids: Eerdmans and Milton Keynes: Paternoster, 2005), 143 n. 27.

17 I am currently working on an academic book on Paul's thorn in the flesh (2 Cor 12:7). You can expect to see that book in publication sometime in the next few years.

18 Posted by dHagar, May 22, 2013 at http://www.urbandictionary.com/define.php?term=people%20pleaser.

19 The ESV and a few other translations renders this verse as though the inChristness portion of the verse relates to the how of the raising, rather than the dying in Jesus. This is possible, though it is difficult to decide whether to go this way or the way the NASB has rendered it, as cited at the beginning of the chapter. Either way, it should be noted that 'through Jesus' and 'in him' (lit. trans. of two parts of the sentence) are emphatic about the importance of union with Christ in the process.

20 I cannot determine the original source of this story.

21 Kenneth Berding, *What Are Spiritual Gifts? Rethinking the Conventional View* (Kregel, 2006).

22 Cicero, Pro Cluentio 15. Cited by Craig Blomberg, *The NIV Application Commentary: 1 Corinthians* (Grand Rapids: Zondervan, 1994), 104 n. 2.

23 I did not make up these nicknames for Euodia and Syntyche. I have heard others refer to them as Odious and Stinky on a number of occasions, but I cannot locate the original source of this play on words, nor even remember where I first heard it.

24 'In Paulo non Paulus vivit, sed Jesus Christus; quare Paulus non in Pauli sed Jesus Christi movetur viseribus.' Bengel, quoted by Barth, and used by Gerald F. Hawthorne, *Philippians, Word Biblical Commentary 43* (Waco, TX.: Word, 1983), 25.

25 Mark Galli, 'Speak the Gospel; Use Deeds When Necessary,' *Christianity Today* 53 (May 2009): 2.

26 See also Maximilian Zerwick, *Biblical Greek*, trans. from fourth Latin ed. by Joseph Smith (Rome: Scripta Pontificii Instituti Biblici, 1963), 13. '…the objective genitive (Paul's love for Christ) does not suffice for, apart from the fact that Paul usually renders the objective-genitive sense by εἰς (cf. Col 1,4), the reason which he adds speaks of the love which Christ manifested for us in dying for all men; nor is the subjective genitive (Christ's love for us) fully satisfactory by itself, because the love in question is a living force working in the spirit of the apostle. In other words, we cannot simply classify this genitive under either heading without neglecting a part of its value. It may also mean the love shown for us by Christ, in His death and resurrection (cf. Rom 4,25!), inasmuch as known (and this through the faith produced in the soul by Christ Himself) and so irresistibly impelling the apostle to return that love.'

27 Thanks especially to Sergiy Tymchenko (director of the program for which I was teaching in Kyiv), who contacted Sergiy Guts (one of my Greek students and director of the spontaneous choir), who contacted Alexey Siniichkin, a historian in St. Petersburg, who confirmed the story and filled in a few historical details. You can hear the song at https://www.youtube.com/watch?v=qlXq_dGXuKg&feature=youtu.be. The translation used in-text is from http://www.zap.org.au/documents/music/gimny-very-khristian/hymns-russian-english/0203-wildly-lifes-billows-are-beating.pdf.

28 The lyrics of 'Onward Christian Soldiers' were written by Sabine Baring-Gould in 1865. The music was composed by Arthur Sullivan in 1871.

FURTHER READING ON
INCHRISTNESS

Do you want to read more about *union with Christ*—what this book has often referred to as *inChristness*? Here are seven helpful resources for you if you are interested in going deeper than the 100 devotionals appearing in this book have already taken you. Please note that I appreciate the work of all these authors—and have benefitted from all of them—though it shouldn't surprise you to learn that I have a few disagreements with each of them on particular points (and, presumably, they with me). Still, I am happy to warmly recommend each of these books. I have ordered these recommended resources from least academic to most academic.

- Rankin Wilbourne, *Union with Christ: The Way to Know and Enjoy God*
- J. Todd Billings, *Union with Christ: Reframing Theology and Ministry for the Church*
- Marcus Peter Johnson, *One with Christ: An Evangelical Theology of Salvation*
- Robert Letham, *Union with Christ: In Scripture, History, and Theology*
- Michael J. Gorman, *Cruciformity: Paul's Narrative Spirituality of the Cross*
- Constantine R. Campbell, *Paul and Union with Christ: An Exegetical and Theological Study*
- Grant Macaskill, *Union with Christ in the New Testament*

QUESTIONS FOR REVIEW

How to Use these Questions: Three Options

1. Use these questions *personally*. After reading a chapter, either spend a few moments thinking about the answers to these questions, or write answers to these questions in a journal.

2. Use these questions in a *small group with preparation*. Assign small-group participants to read a certain number of devotional readings (say, seven readings a week, that is, one for each day of the week), and then use the review questions as starter questions for your discussions together.

3. Use these questions in a *small group with no preparation*. These devotional readings are short enough that you could come together with no preparation, read one reading aloud (which will take about five minutes), then discuss the questions together. When you have finished discussing a chapter, you could read the next section aloud…and so on until your time is finished.

Introduction

*   Why did this book need to be written according to the author?

*   Why did the author claim at the beginning that writing this book was 'deeply personal' for him?

Chapter 1: *InChristness*

*   Compared to the other teachings of Paul in his letters, how important is Paul's teaching about what this book calls *inChristness*?

*   What does it mean to be 'in' someone, according to Paul? What does it mean to be 'in Christ'? What sorts of problems do you think we face when we forget that we are 'in Christ'?

Chapter 2: Access to God in Christ

- The word 'access' in English means that someone is permitted to enter a place where he hasn't been permitted previously. But in Romans 5:2 it means a bit more than just that. According to this reading, what is that extra meaning, and why does it matter?

- Why is it important for Christians who feel distant from God to know that they have access to God through Jesus Christ?

Chapter 3: Dead to Sin in Christ

- What is the main difference between a believer in Christ and a non-believer when it comes to overcoming sin?

- What metaphors (word pictures) does Paul use to communicate that the power of sin has been broken in our lives? How do these metaphors help you to think about overcoming sin?

Chapter 4: Alive to God in Christ

- What spiritual truth does the metaphor of being raised with Christ communicate?

- What do you need to do if you have trouble really believing that you have died to your old life and been raised to a new life in Christ?

Chapter 5: Not Under Law through Christ

- Are Christians under the Old Testament law?

- How does knowing about our relationship to the Old Testament law make a difference in the way we live our lives in Christ?

Chapter 6: No Condemnation in Christ

- How much of our condemnation was taken care of through the cross of Jesus? What practical difference does knowing the answer to this question make in your life?

- For those of us who often replay condemning messages in our heads, what does this chapter suggest we should do about those messages? How might your life look different if you did this as a habit?

Chapter 7: Co-heirs with Christ

- What are some of the implications of sharing in Christ's inheritance?
- Is it more common for you to view yourself as part of Christ's family, or do you more commonly view yourself as a servant of Christ? What difference does having the perspective that you are a co-heir with Christ make?

Chapter 8: Mediation of Christ

- How does this chapter describe the 'torpedo' we have in God's courtroom?
- How does knowing about the mediation of Christ help you when you pray? How does this compare to the way you have prayed in the past?

Chapter 9: Triumph through Christ

- Are we conquerors, or not? Are we victorious in Christ, or not? Is the answer to this question only 'yes' or 'no'? Explain.
- What difference does it make in our lives to know about Christ triumphing over Satan on the cross?

Chapter 10: No Separation in Christ

- When have you most experienced feelings of separation?
- How does knowing about the truth that nothing can separate you from the love of Christ make a difference in how you live life? How do our 'feelings' hinder us from believing the truth that nothing can separate us from God's love?

Chapter 11: Belonging to Christ

- Do you ever struggle with feelings of not belonging? If you do, what do you think has contributed to these feelings?

- How does it help you to know that you *belong* to Christ?

Chapter 12: Justified in Christ

- What does it mean to be justified in Christ?

- Do we sometimes live like we haven't been justified? Can you think of any real-life examples of times we live as though we haven't been justified?

Chapter 13: Slaves but Free in Christ

- How does viewing ourselves as slaves of Christ help us in our spiritual lives?

- How does viewing ourselves as freedpersons in Christ help us in our spiritual lives? Which of these two (slaves of Christ or freedperson in Christ) do you think you need to focus upon more?

Chapter 14: Future Resurrection in Christ

- In what ways does our future resurrection described in the Bible differ from Plato's view of the afterlife?

- How does looking forward to our future resurrection help us to live the lives that God wants us to live now?

Chapter 15: Veil Removed in Christ

- How is reading the Old Testament, including the law of Moses, similar to trying to understand George Orwell's book *Animal Farm*?

- What do we miss if we only read the Old Testament as a collection of laws and stories from Israel's history?

Chapter 16: A New Creation in Christ

- What is biblical authenticity?

- What difference does it make to know that we are new creations in Christ?

Chapter 17: Identity in Christ

- What do we learn about a Christian's identity from the story of the martyrdom of Polycarp?
- What is the difference between how a Christian should view his or her identity and how others in our generation often view identity?

Chapter 18: Christ in Us

- Union with Christ is not only about being 'in Christ,' it also is about Christ being in us. How does Jesus dwell in us?
- What are some of the insights you found helpful from the allegory of opening our house (our lives) to Jesus?

Chapter 19: Substitution of Christ

- What is meant when the Bible describes Jesus as our substitute?
- Why do you think Christians should spend time thinking about the substitutionary death of Jesus?

Chapter 20: Promises in Christ

- How do we know that keeping promises is important to God?
- How does the theme of God keeping His promises impact the way we live?

Chapter 21: Baptized into Christ

- What does water baptism symbolize?
- What does it mean to say that we have died, been buried, and been raised with Christ?

Chapter 22: Clothed with Christ

- What spiritual truths does the metaphor of being clothed with Christ represent?

- If we have been clothed with Christ, how should we respond to this truth?

Chapter 23: Blessed in Christ

- What does it mean to be blessed in Christ with every spiritual blessing in the heavenly places?
- Why do you think that Paul wanted us to know about the spiritual blessings we have received in Christ?

Chapter 24: Chosen in Christ

- Why is adoption a good metaphor for explaining what it means to be chosen by God?
- How should we respond to the truth that we were chosen in Christ?

Chapter 25: Forgiven in Christ

- On what basis did God forgive the sins of those who put their faith in Him? What is the extent of that forgiveness?
- What does this chapter suggest is the proper response to the truth that we have been forgiven in Christ? Do you find it easy to respond in this way?

Chapter 26: Seated with Christ

- Why do you think that Paul first wrote about Christ being seated before he wrote about us being seated with Him?
- What does it mean that we are seated with Christ? What difference does it make in the way we live?

Chapter 27: Grace in Christ

- What is the relationship between grace and giving thanks?
- How can you implement more thankfulness for God's grace this week?

Chapter 28: Mystery of Christ

- What is the mystery of Christ? Was it totally unknown in the past?

- What are the implications of the answer to this first question? How does it impact how we relate to one another?

Chapter 29: Found in Christ

- Why did Paul write about being 'found' in Christ rather than 'finding' Christ? What did Paul mean when he said that we wanted to be found in Christ?

- How does longing for the future help us in the way we live now?

Chapter 30: Upward Call of God in Christ

- What was Paul probably picturing when he wrote about the upward call of God in Christ?

- After you have gone to be with Christ and had an opportunity to look back on your life, what does this chapter suggest you might notice? How does this encourage you?

Chapter 31: Redemption in Christ

- What three 'biblical bells' should go off in your head when you hear the word 'redemption'?

- What have we been redeemed *out of*? How does this impact our lives?

Chapter 32: Rooted in Christ

- Why is rootedness in Christ such a powerful metaphor?

- What are some examples of ways that being rooted in Christ might affect your life?

Chapter 33: Circumcised by Christ

- What is the Old Testament background to Paul's statement that we have been spiritually circumcised?

- How does knowing about this truth help you when facing a temptation to sin?

Chapter 34: Hidden with Christ in God

- What does it mean that we are hidden with Christ in God?

- When are you most likely to feel insecure? How does this picture of being hidden with Christ in God help people who feel insecure?

DAILY LIFE *IN CHRIST*

Chapter 35: Conformed to the Image of Christ

- The purpose of this book is to connect *inChristness* with daily life. How does a verse that mentions predestination (Rom. 8:29) connect to daily life?

- God's goal is to conform you to the image of Christ. How does thinking about this truth help you when facing trials and suffering?

Chapter 36: Telling the Truth in Christ

- How does *inChristness* relate to truth-telling?

- Why do people normally lie? Why is lying such a problem for relationships?

Chapter 37: Boasting in Christ

- What are some things that Paul 'boasted' about that were good things? What did he 'boast' about more than anything else?

- Can you think of any examples from your own life when you have inappropriately boasted? Can you think of any examples from your life when you have boasted in the appropriate way?

Chapter 38: Work in Christ

- How does it help you to know that all work should be done *in Christ*?

- How would your work look different from how it does now if Jesus were your co-worker?

Chapter 39: Sanctification in Christ

- How are two ways that the Apostle Paul uses the word 'sanctification'? How do you think those two ways relate to each other?
- According to this chapter, why should a Christian strive for holiness?

Chapter 40: Fellowship with Christ

- What does it mean that we have been called into fellowship with Christ?
- What does it look like in practice to live a life of fellowship with Christ?

Chapter 41: The Mind of Christ

- What does it mean to say that a Christian has the 'mind of Christ'?
- What do you find most challenging about growing into this new way of thinking referred to by Paul as 'the mind of Christ'?

Chapter 42: Sexual Purity in Christ

- What is the key thing highlighted in this chapter that needs to be done by the person who wants to resist sexual temptation?
- What are some other things that are helpful in the fight for sexual purity?

Chapter 43: Imitators of Christ

- How does the theme of *imitation of Christ* intersect with the theme of *inChristness*?
- When you read the stories in the Bible about the life of Jesus, what aspects of His life do you find yourself especially wanting to imitate?

Chapter 44: Hope in Christ

- How is biblical hope different from the way we often use the word 'hope' in English?

- How does biblical hope keep us from losing hope?

Chapter 45: Sharing Christ's Sufferings

- Do Christians suffer less than those who don't know Christ? How common is suffering for Christians?

- Why do you think Christians often find comfort from meditating on the truth that Jesus suffered before them?

Chapter 46: Comfort in Christ

- What is another (common) translation of the Greek word that normally gets translated as 'comfort' in 2 Corinthians 1:3-7? Why is it helpful to know about this other common translation of this word?

- How does knowing that you are *in Christ* help you when you face dark and difficult periods in your life?

Chapter 47: Glory of Christ

- What does it mean for someone to be the 'glory of Christ'?

- What specific ways can you give glory to Christ?

Chapter 48: Thought-Life in Christ

- Why do you think that it is so hard to control our thoughts? Why do our thoughts wander so easily in unholy and meaningless directions?

- What can we do to 'take every thought captive to obey Christ'?

Chapter 49: Sincere Devotion to Christ

- What things are most likely to divert you from a pure and sincere devotion to Christ?

- Have you ever used a Scripture verse as a focal point throughout the day? If you have, how has doing that helped you?

Chapter 50: Weakness and Power in Christ

- Can you think of any examples in your life or in the life of anyone close to you where you have witnessed the truth that power is perfected in weakness (2 Cor. 12:9)?
- What do you think is the process by which power increases through weakness? Does spiritual power automatically increase in everyone who is weak?

Chapter 51: Pleasing Christ

- Do you find yourself expending a lot of emotional energy trying to please others?
- What is the difference between being a people-pleaser and serving out of love?

Chapter 52: Faith in Christ

- 'Just believe' is a common expression in our broader culture. How is biblical faith different from what many people think of as simply believing?
- This chapter offers some examples of what faith might look like in practice. What are some of those examples? Can you think of other examples?

Chapter 53: Formation in Christ

- What is spiritual formation? What can we learn about formation from Galatians 4:19?
- What is God's role in spiritual formation? What is our role?

Chapter 54: Thankfulness in Christ

- This chapter claims that thankfulness is one way of describing the entire Christian life. What do you think is meant by the claim that thankfulness can describe the whole of the Christian life?

- How do you think you can become a more thankful person?

Chapter 55: Growth and Maturity in Christ

- What are some signs that a Christian is growing and maturing in Christ?

- Do you think that you are in a season of growing and maturing? Why or why not?

Chapter 56: Learning Christ

- What is the difference between learning about Christ and learning Christ?

- Is there anything you can do to make sure that you are continuing to learn Christ?

Chapter 57: The Name of Jesus

- What does it mean to pray, or to do anything else for that matter, in the *name* of Jesus?

- Why is it important to know about the authority you have in and through the name of Jesus? Can you think of any instances when knowing about this authority would be important?

Chapter 58: Humility in Christ

- What does our humility have to do with our union with Christ?

- What are some obvious reasons why we should concern ourselves with being humble?

Chapter 59: Rejoicing in Christ

- What is the difference between joy and happiness?

- Can you describe a time in your life when you have experienced more Christian joy than you are currently? What was different about that period?

Chapter 60: Everything as Loss to Gain Christ

- What did Paul mean when he wrote that he counted everything as loss in order to gain Christ?
- What helps you stay focused on Christ?

Chapter 61: Knowing Christ

- Is there a difference between knowing about Christ and knowing Christ?
- This chapter includes a lot of exclamation points. Paul's own comments in Philippians 3 are vibrant and passionate. Do you ever struggle when you hear others passionately describing their lives in Christ? How do you find yourself relating to zeal in others?

Chapter 62: Peace of Christ

- This chapter suggests that a believer in Christ can experience both sorrow and peace at the same time. Have you ever seen both of these working together in your own life or in the life of another Christian you know?
- How has Christ's peace been present during a time of sorrow in your life?

Chapter 63: Contentment through Christ

- What does Paul mean when he claims, 'I can do all things through him who strengthens me' (Phil. 4:13)?
- Would you describe yourself as a content person? How do you think God might want you to respond to the topic of this chapter? Can you think of any specific ways?

Chapter 64: Needs supplied in Christ

- Philippians 4:19 reads: 'And my God will supply every need of yours according to his riches in glory in Christ Jesus.' What is a *need*?
- How have you seen God provide for your needs?

Chapter 65: Walking in Christ

- Why do you think Paul used walking to describe living life in Christ? Why choose walking and not something else?
- How might a day in your life look different if Jesus physically walked next to you throughout the day?

Chapter 66: Life is Christ

- How might things look different if you viewed Christ as your entire reason for existence?
- Do you have any desire to adjust your 'bucket list' after reading this chapter?

Chapter 67: Physically Dying in Christ

- What is the difference between dying in Christ and apart from Christ?
- Have you ever felt afraid of dying? How might the truths you've read about in this chapter help you deal with fear of death?

COMMUNITY AND MISSION *IN CHRIST*

Chapter 68: One Body in Christ

- This chapter is about unity. But are there ever times when we should not seek for unity with others who call themselves Christians?
- Is your natural tendency to work toward unity or against unity? In light of your tendencies, is there anything you think the Lord would want you to adjust after reading this chapter?

Chapter 69: Churches in Christ

- Why is it important to be a part of a local church?

- Do you think God wants you to make any adjustments in the amount and/or quality of your involvement in the local church to which you are connected?

Chapter 70: No Distinctions in Christ

- How might meditating on the shared *inChristness* of Christians help us to address injustices toward varying ethnicities and cultures?

- How much have you thought about your own ethnic and cultural background? How can you grow to have greater sensitivity about your own cultural privileges and develop a heart of love and compassion toward others who are different from you?

Chapter 71: Ministry Roles in Christ

- Does Paul focus on Christians *having* abilities to do particular ministries, or does he focus more on encouraging people to *serve* in God-appointed ministries?

- What ministries are you currently involved in that are building Christ's church and extending God's kingdom work in the world? Are there any ministries that you should be doing that you are not currently doing?

Chapter 72: Hospitality in Christ

- What did we learn in this chapter about the importance and practice of hospitality during the first century A.D. when Paul wrote his letters?

- Can you think of any ways in which God might want you to grow into being a more hospitable person?

Chapter 73: Spiritual Parenting in Christ

- What does it mean to be a spiritual parent in Christ?

- Can you think of anyone with whom God would want you to do some spiritual parenting?

Chapter 74: Sinning Against Christ

- How do we sin against Christ when we sin against a Christian brother or sister?
- Think about the Christians you know. Can you think of anyone against whom you have sinned in any way and haven't made it right? What do you think you need to do to make it right?

Chapter 75: Communion in Christ

- Why do we sometimes call the Lord's Supper 'communion'?
- Is there anything in this chapter that might help you understand why sharing the Lord's Supper is important?

Chapter 76: Church Discipline in Christ

- What did you learn about church discipline from reading this chapter?
- Modern Christians are not usually fond of church discipline. Do you think church discipline is important? Why or why not?

Chapter 77: Loving Others in Christ

- What is Christian love?
- How can we grow into loving others more?

Chapter 78: Forgiving Others in Christ

- Why should Christians take responsibility for forgiving others who have wronged them?
- Is there anyone that comes to mind that you have not yet forgiven? What should you do if you are really struggling to forgive someone?

Chapter 79: Generosity through Christ

- This chapter explains a bit about a key ministry of Paul that many people don't know about. What did you learn about that ministry? What did you learn about the Macedonians' response to that ministry?

- What is your current approach to sharing money and resources? What practical steps might you take to become more generous?

Chapter 80: Family in Christ

- How common was it for people in the first century to view people outside of their natural families as though they were family members?

- When have you benefitted from being part of God's spiritual family? Can you think of some ways to express the truth that you are part of a spiritual family?

Chapter 81: Agreement in Christ

- Does agreeing in Christ mean that we always share the same opinion?

- Take a moment and consider whether argumentativeness is a characteristic of your life. How can argumentative people become less argumentative?

Chapter 82: Affection of Christ

- Why is it that Christians, even Christians who have never even previously met, often feel such affection for one another?

- How can you grow into being more affectionate toward other Christians?

Chapter 83: Word of Christ

- What does Paul mean by 'the word of Christ' in Colossians 3:16?

- How can we cultivate a church environment where people are excited to converse about Christ in and outside the church building?

Chapter 84: Church Leadership in Christ

- Would you describe yourself as a critical person in relationship to your church leaders? Recognizing that some evaluation is proper and necessary, do you think that you are currently doing what would honor the Lord in this area?

- If you are in any sort of leadership role in your church, how much do the opinions of others affect you? Are you leaning into your *inChristness* when you face criticisms?

Chapter 85: Welcoming Christ

- How might your actions change if you knew that the needy person before you was an angel—or even Christ Jesus Himself?

- How does someone become a more welcoming person?

Chapter 86: Speaking in Christ

- Is it possible to 'speak' the gospel only by living it out in your actions? How important are actions? How important is speaking for communicating the good news of Jesus with others?

- How does it help you in your interactions with others to know that all speaking should be done *in Christ*?

Chapter 87: Letters from Christ

- Did Paul think that he needed letters of recommendation for the church in Corinth? Why or why not?

- What do you think people 'read' when they look at the letter that is your life? Is this what you would like them to 'read'?

Chapter 88: Created in Christ for Good Works

- What are some biblical examples of people doing good works as a result of their relationship to Christ? What are some good modern examples?
- How would you like to be remembered after you die?

Chapter 89: Power and Wisdom of God in Christ

- This chapter explains one of the reasons why Paul sometimes was criticized in Corinth. What was that reason?
- Have you ever met someone who was overly obsessed with miracles? Have you ever met someone who was too easily influenced by persuasive preachers? How can a Christian find proper balance in these areas?

Chapter 90: Open Doors in Christ

- What was an 'open door' according to Paul? Did an open door mean that there would not be any difficulties? How do we know?
- Are there any doors that appear to be open for you, but that you are reticent about stepping through?

Chapter 91: Fragrance of Christ

- If we could just package the message about Christ differently, do you think that people in the world would automatically receive it? What are some of the reasons that people reject the gospel message?
- What would you like your life to 'smell' like?

Chapter 92: Controlled by the Love of Christ

- What does the expression 'the love of Christ' in 2 Corinthians 5:14 mean?
- What are some of the main things that motivate you—positive and negative?

Chapter 93: Reconciliation through Christ

- Why is the story about the relationship of the Apostle Paul to John Mark so powerful?

- In light of the story of Paul and Mark, take a moment and consider whether there might be someone from whom you are estranged and with whom you need to make an attempt (or one more attempt) at reconciliation. Is there anyone who just now came to mind?

Chapter 94: Ambassadors for Christ

- What are some characteristics of ambassadors that connect with our being ambassadors for Christ?

- Can you think of a neighbor, co-worker, or friend whom you would like to talk to about Christ?

Chapter 95: Fools for Christ

- Why were Paul and his co-workers sometimes viewed as foolish?

- Have you ever been viewed as foolish simply because you are a Christian (not because you were being unkind or insensitive)?

Chapter 96: Spiritual Warfare in Christ

- What is spiritual warfare?

- What should you do if you think you are experiencing an attack from Satan and his demons?

Chapter 97: Persecution in Christ

- How aware are you of the widespread persecution of Christians around the world? (If you're not very aware, do an online search for the ministries *Open Doors* or *Voice of the Martyrs* and learn some more.)

- If you ever find yourself facing persecution as a Christian, how should you respond?

Chapter 98: Confidence in Christ

- Do you feel nervous about sharing your faith in Jesus Christ with others?

- What can you do to overcome your fear of sharing Christ with others?

Chapter 99: Soldiers of Christ

- The Christian's battle is against whom or what? Whom is it *not* against?

- What are some benefits of viewing ourselves as soldiers?

Chapter 100: Ministry Results through Christ

- Are you responsible for producing the results of ministry?

- How does knowing the answer to this question help you when you're in the middle of intense ministry?

Bonus Chapter: Abiding in Christ

- What is the source of Paul's extensive teaching about *inChristness*? In other words, from whom does he get it?

- What does it mean to 'abide in Christ' (John 15)?

SCRIPTURE INDEX

Christian Focus Publications

Our mission statement –

STAYING FAITHFUL

In dependence upon God we seek to impact the world through literature faithful to His infallible Word, the Bible. Our aim is to ensure that the Lord Jesus Christ is presented as the only hope to obtain forgiveness of sin, live a useful life and look forward to heaven with Him.

Our Books are published in four imprints:

CHRISTIAN
FOCUS

popular works including biographies, commentaries, basic doctrine and Christian living.

CHRISTIAN
HERITAGE

books representing some of the best material from the rich heritage of the church.

MENTOR

books written at a level suitable for Bible College and seminary students, pastors, and other serious readers. The imprint includes commentaries, doctrinal studies, examination of current issues and church history.

CF4•K

children's books for quality Bible teaching and for all age groups: Sunday school curriculum, puzzle and activity books; personal and family devotional titles, biographies and inspirational stories – Because you are never too young to know Jesus!

Christian Focus Publications Ltd,
Geanies House, Fearn, Ross-shire,
IV20 1TW, Scotland, United Kingdom.
www.christianfocus.com